GO BANG
TAMBOU

A Play
by
PHILIP KING

SAMUEL · FRENCH

LONDON
NEW YORK TORONTO SYDNEY HOLLYWOOD

© 1970 BY PHILIP KING

This play is fully protected under the copyright laws of the British Commonwealth of Nations, the United States of America, and all countries of the Berne and Universal Copyright Conventions.

All rights are strictly reserved.

It is an infringement of the copyright to give any public performance or reading of this play either in its entirety or in the form of excerpts without the prior consent of the copyright owners. No part of this publication may be transmitted, stored in a retrieval system, or reproduced in any form or by any means, electronic, mechanical, photocopying, manuscript, typescript, recording, or otherwise, without the prior permission of the copyright owners.

SAMUEL FRENCH LTD, 26 SOUTHAMPTON STREET, STRAND, LONDON WC2, or their authorized agents, issue licences to amateurs to give performances of this play on payment of a fee. **The fee must be paid, and the licence obtained, before a performance is given.**

Licences are issued subject to the understanding that it shall be made clear in all advertising matter that the audience will witness an amateur performance; and that the names of the authors of plays shall be included on all announcements and on all programmes.

The royalty fee indicated below is subject to contract and subject to variation at the sole discretion of Samuel French Ltd.

Basic fee for each and every performance by amateurs in the British Isles	£6	
In theatres or halls seating 600 or more the fee will be subject to negotiation.		

In territories overseas the fee quoted above may not apply. Application must be made to our local authorized agents, or if there is no such agent, to Samuel French Ltd, London.

PR
6021
.I275
G6

GB 573 01217 2

LiT

GO BANG YOUR TAMBOURINE

David Armstrong
Bess Jones
Thomas Armstrong
Major Webber

The action of the play passes in the living-room of a small house in a street of working-class dwellings in a Midland town.

ACT 1
    Scene 1   An afternoon in late September
    Scene 2   Evening; a month later

ACT II
    Scene 1   Evening; three weeks later
    Scene 2   Late Sunday afternoon; about
               three weeks later

ACT III   Early evening; two days later

Time—the present

GO BANG YOUR TAMBOURINE

ACT I

Scene 1

The living-room of a small house in a street of working-class dwellings in a town in the Midlands. An afternoon in late September.

The room is quite small, with a front door opening directly on to the street, another to the kitchen, and a third revealing the turn of a narrow staircase. There is a club fender in front of the fireplace, with Rexine-covered seats at either end. A window looks out on the street to one side of the front door, and there is a light switch on the other side. The furniture, the main items of which are a largish table, a sofa and a dresser, is nondescript and not new. The room is spotlessly clean and tidy.

When the CURTAIN *rises, the room is empty. There is not much light, as the blind is drawn at the window. After a pause, the street door opens and David Armstrong and his father, Thomas Armstrong, are seen on the threshold. David is a lad of nineteen; inclined to thinness, pale-faced and sensitive. He wears a Salvation Army uniform under a dark mackintosh. Thomas is a man of forty-five. He is the reverse of David—broad-shouldered, rugged, and coarsely good-looking. He wears a dark suit, black tie and a mackintosh. He is brusque of manner, and inclined to bursts of irritability and impatience. David, on the other hand, is of a shy, quiet disposition, and decidedly reticent in his manner towards Thomas. He is never rude to him, only 'distant'. It soon becomes obvious that there is no 'father and son' affection between the two. They are ill at ease in each other's company.*

After the door is opened, David half-gestures to Thomas to go in first.

Thomas (*with a touch of impatience*) No, no. You . . .

David does not move

Oh well, age before beauty, I suppose. (*He steps into the room*)

David, taking his Yale key from the lock in the door, follows Thomas in, closes the door, then shakes his Salvation Army cap and hangs it on the hook behind the door

(*Still somewhat impatiently*) Can't we have a bit of daylight on the scene?

David (*quietly*) I'll . . . (*He moves to the window and lets the blind up, and stands looking out*)

Thomas Morbid idea—drawing blinds for a death. Thought that'd gone out years ago. (*He moves to the fireplace, rubbing his hands*) Thank God for a fire! Perishin' cold standin' about in that cemetery. (*He removes*

1

his mackintosh then looks across towards David. With some irritation)
Aren't you going to take yours off?

David, who has hardly heard all Thomas has said, turns

David H'mm?

Thomas You don't want to stand about in that soppin' wet mac, or you'll
be the next to . . . (*He pulls up quickly. He throws his own wet mac over
the back of the armchair*)

*David moves down at once, though not quickly, and removes Thomas's mac
from the chair. Thomas notices this but says nothing*

David (*quietly*) I'll put 'em in the back kitchen; they can drip in there.
(*He moves to the kitchen door, then hesitates. Again quietly*) You—you
won't be wanting yours for a bit?

Thomas (*after a look*) Wantin' to get rid of me already?

David shakes his head

If you are, you've only got to say so.

David (*quietly*) Won't be a minute.

David goes off into the kitchen

*Thomas looks after him, almost angrily, for a moment, then begins to look
around the room, and is obviously not very impressed with what he sees.
He produces a pipe and tobacco pouch and slowly fills his pipe as he looks
round. He then produces matches, lights one, hesitates, looking towards
the kitchen door, before lighting his pipe. He then moves around, still
surveying the room disparagingly. He is by the front door when his eyes
fall on David's Salvation Army cap on the hook behind it. He takes the
cap down, twists it around in his hand, then slips it on to his own head for
a moment. Removing it, he glances at it again before almost hurling it
back on to the hook, with a grunt of disapproval and exasperation. He is
wandering down to the fireplace when his eyes fall on a black box, actually
a cornet case, on the floor by the wall. He looks at it, then prods it, curiously, with his foot*

*David returns quietly from the kitchen while Thomas is prodding the box.
He stands watching him*

*Thomas, sensing David's presence, turns, looks at him, then at the box, then
back to David—obviously expecting to be told what is in it. David, how-
ever, offers no explanation, but stands looking at Thomas. There is no
resentment on his face—it is almost expressionless. Thomas returns
David's look for quite a while*

Thomas (*at last*) Aren't you going to ask me to sit down?

David (*quietly*) I'm sorry. (*He gestures for Thomas to sit*)

Thomas (*sitting in the armchair*) Place hasn't changed much since I left.
Still the same old furniture. But then—your mother never worried
much about her—her (*almost sardonically*) earthly home, did she? More
concerned about . . .

David (*cutting in*) I've put the kettle on for a cup of tea. Would you like
something to eat with it? A poached egg or . . .

2

Thomas (*aware of David's cutting in*) No thanks. A cup of tea'll do me fine.
David The kettle won't be long.

There is a slight pause

Thomas Were you surprised to see me at the funeral?
David (*with the slightest shrug*) I wondered whether you'd come.
Thomas I suppose I ought to've come as soon as I heard from you——
David There was no need . . .
Thomas (*deliberately going on as if David had not spoken*) —but there was
a special job on at the works which had to be finished by last night—*and*
we had to work late on it. That's why I couldn't get away from Nottingham until this morning, and why I couldn't come along here to the
house first. Went straight from the train to the—Salvation Army place.
In any case I expect I'd only've been in the way here if I *had* come.
(*After a slight pause*) Incidentally, I didn't know the Salvation Army
buried their own dead. I thought they had to be taken to a proper
church. (*He waits for David to speak, but then goes on*) Oh, and by the
way—the undertaker's bill—when you get it, you'd better send it on
to me.
David (*quietly, but not offensively*) You needn't worry about that.
Thomas (*at once taking umbrage*) I'm not 'worrying' about it. I'm just
telling you to send it on to me.
David (*quietly*) Mother had a small insurance—about sixty pounds—
that'll pay for the funeral. If not, I can . . . (*His voice tails away*)
Thomas (*after looking at him for a moment*) You do hate me, don't you?
David (*almost violently*) No! I don't hate you! (*Then almost a murmur*)
I don't hate anybody. It's wrong to hate people.
Thomas (*with silencing gesture*) All right! All right! Don't let's have any
sermons. (*After a slight pause*) There are a few things we ought to talk
about I suppose, so let's . . .
David (*quickly, and somewhat nervously*) I'll bring the tea in before we
start. (*He moves to the kitchen door*)
Thomas (*irritably*) Now look . . .

But David has gone into the kitchen

*Thomas, obviously annoyed, rises, and again moves around—to the fireplace.
He notices a framed postcard sized photograph (David and his mother) on
the mantelpiece. He takes it down, looks at it, then with an exasperated sigh,
replaces it. He looks round again disconsolately then takes out a watch,
consults it, then re-lighting his pipe, goes to the armchair and almost throws
himself into it*

(*To himself, quietly*) Oh hell! (*He wriggles down into the chair and smokes
moodily*)

*David enters from the kitchen, carrying a tray on which are tea things
for two*

(*With an attempt at brightness*) Ah! The cup that cheers, eh?

David (*after putting milk in the cups*) D'you take sugar?
Thomas Just one—ta!

David pours tea, then takes Thomas's cup across to him

David I hope it's all right. (*He goes back to the table, draws a straight-backed chair from under it, sits, facing Thomas, and takes a drink of tea*)
Thomas (*after having taken some tea*) It's fine. Fine! You make a good cuppa, son.

There is a silence while they both drink again

(*At last*) I was just looking at that photograph up there! (*He nods towards it*) You and your mother.
David (*quietly*) Oh!
Thomas Not bad—of both of you. When was it taken?
David About a year ago. We'd both just got new uniforms.
Thomas (*with rather heavy humour*) Fancied yourselves a bit, eh?

David gives a dutiful half-smile

Well now—(*He clears his throat*)—I—I thought everything went off very well this afternoon. It was lucky that storm holding off until it was all over. (*After a slight pause*) And I was surprised to see so many people there. Were they all friends of your mother's or had they just come for a sing-song?
David (*quietly*) Mum had lots of friends.
Thomas You mean in the . . . ?
David Yes.
Thomas And how long have you been—caught up with it?
David (*resenting the way Thomas has put the question*) What do you mean?
Thomas You know damn' well what I mean. How long have you been in the Salvation Army?
David (*with restraint*) I joined just after you—went away.
Thomas (*with a little laugh*) H'mm! I'll bet your mother didn't waste much time before she got you along there.
David (*rising; deliberately*) More tea?
Thomas What? Oh, yes.

David takes his cup and pours tea

(*Watching him*) Let's see—*how* old are you now?
David (*pouring*) Nineteen.
Thomas (*reflectively*) Nineteen . . . !
David (*not with bitterness*) I was just turned fifteen when you left Mother, and . . .
Thomas And went off with another woman—go on, say it.

David brings his tea to him, silently

I don't know what your mother told you, but——
David (*with a break in his voice*) Mum never . . . (*He runs a hand over his eyes*)

4

Thomas (*again ignoring David's interruption*) —but you might as well hear my side of it. Sit down.

David I don't want to . . .

Thomas Sit down.

David sits, partly turned from Thomas

It wasn't just because of Doris that I cleared off. I'd've had to go in any case, 'cos I couldn't've stuck it here any longer. For years your mother and me had been getting on each other's nerves and we'd—God knows what might've happened. (*Quickly*) I'm not saying it was her fault any more than mine—it was just that we didn't see eye to eye—about—well about anything. I know when you're married you're supposed to take each other for better or worse, but—I can't swallow that. When you don't get on together what's the point of going on—making each other's life a misery day in, day out? We just weren't suited to each other. *I* realized that—even before you were born; so did your mother, though she'd never admit it. Then—when you arrived—I think we both thought things might improve, but—it didn't work out that way. They only went from bad to worse—till I got to the stage . . . Then—I met Doris, and . . .

David (*quietly*) Will you—marry her now?

Thomas (*somewhat surprised*) Doris? We . . . (*He pulls up sharply*) Never mind about her. We've other matters to think of at the moment—you and me. (*After a slight pause, then more business-like, and anxious to change the subject*) Er—I don't suppose your mother left a will, did she?

David A . . . ? No, I don't think—in fact I'm sure she didn't. I've—been through her things. I had to, to . . .

Thomas No. I don't suppose she'd have anything much to leave—don't see how she could have—not really. (*Then almost aggressively*) You *do* know what I sent her every week?

David Yes.

Thomas (*after a look at him*) Are there—are there any papers I ought to see to? You said something about an insurance policy. Would you like me to deal with that?

David (*going to a drawer in the dresser and taking out a small bundle of papers*) I put what papers there are all together. (*He brings them down and hands them to Thomas*) That's all there are.

David moves away, and again his hand passes over his eyes. He sits at the table, then slowly covers his face with his hands

Thomas (*not aware of David; going through papers, not deliberately casually, but rather matter of fact*) Oh, she *had* a Post Office Bank Book then! (*He opens the book*) Nine pounds . . . H'm! Oh, and here's the insurance. (*He opens the policy and reads it for a moment or two*) Yes . . . . ! Yes, well I'll see to this—and I'll have it made payable to you—*and* the Post Office Savings. Between them they should just about cover the funeral. (*Looking at another paper*) What . . . ? Oh, marriage lines. (*He glances at these briefly*) Yes—well—(*casually, but not deliberately so*)—no point in my taking them. (*He drops the marriage certificate absently to the*

5

floor) Doesn't seem to be much else. (*Looking at one or two envelopes*)
Letters—from her sister in Australia by the look of 'em. (*He throws
them on top of the marriage certificate*) And that's the lot, seemingly.
(*He puts the insurance policy and Post Office Book into his pocket. He
now looks across at David and sees he is distressed. Almost gruffly, but
quietly, as he moves to him and gives him a light pat on the back*) Come
on, now; come on. Pull yourself together. I know it isn't very pleasant
having to go into these things, but it's something that's got to be done.
(*He moves to the fireplace*) Now there's nothing else anywhere, is there?

David (*rising*) No. (*He runs a hand over his eyes, then braces himself*)

Thomas (*his eyes falling on the black box again*) Er—this box . . .

David (*vaguely*) What box?

Thomas (*indicating it*) This one. Looks—kind of—important. (*With a
half grin*) What d'you keep in it—the family jewels?

David No. It's a cornet.

Thomas (*blankly*) A what?

David (*quietly*) A cornet.

Thomas (*still puzzled*) A cor——? (*Then understanding*) Oh I know what
you mean! A sort of bugle—trumpet thing.

David Sort of.

Thomas H'mm! (*He looks at the box for a moment*) Mind if I have a look
at it?

*David goes and picks up the box, almost gently, undoes the catches and
carefully takes out a highly polished, silver-plated cornet*

(*As the cornet comes into view; admiringly*) Blimey! (*Suddenly*) It isn't
yours, is it?

David (*quietly*) Yes.

Thomas H'm! It's a smasher, isn't it? Let's . . . (*He holds out a hand*)

David hands him the cornet

(*Inspecting it*) Yeah! A real beaut! Not that I know anything about
these things, but if looks are anything to go by . . . ! (*His fingers on the
stops*) You press these knobs up and down, don't you?

David Yes.

Thomas H'm! Must've cost you a pretty penny, this.

David (*after a slight pause*) Mum gave it to me—(*quietly*)—for my last
birthday . . .

Thomas (*uncomfortably*) Oh! I see!

David It was one of her ambitions—to see me in the band.

Thomas The Salvation . . . ?

David Yes.

Thomas *Are* you in it?

David I'm only just learning to play. The Bandmaster at the Citadel—he's
teaching me.

Thomas Can you knock a tune out of it yet?

David Not properly. I can just about manage *Bluebells of Scotland*, and
There is a Green . . . — a hymn.

Thomas Ah well! Keep on practisin' and you might turn out to be a real

top-notcher on it—another Eddie Calvert! Well, you never know, do
you? Get with one of them top line bands and you're in the money,
aren't you?

Thomas looks towards David, who lowers his eyes

(*Irritably*) A damn sight more sensible than wasting your time blowing
out hymns at street corners and playing hell with everybody's Sunday
afternoon. (*Surlily*) Here—(*thrusting the cornet at David*)—take it!

*David takes the cornet and stands looking at it for a moment or two.
Thomas moves away, lighting his pipe. Seeing David's absorption in the
cornet he throws the match away irritably*

(*With a gesture towards the cornet; irritably*) Look . . . forget that for a
minute or two, will you?

David lays the cornet on the table

Let's get back to—business. We've got you to think about, haven't we?
What's going to happen to *you* now?

David (*quietly, without offence*) You don't have to worry about me.

Thomas (*with an irritated burst*) Don't keep telling me I don't have to
worry about this, and don't have to worry about that! Dammit, you're
my son, aren't you? Course I've got to 'worry' about you. (*After a slight
pause*) You're—at work now, of course.

David Yes.

Thomas Where? (*Then quickly*) You're *not* with the—(*gesturing towards
his uniform*)—not full time, are you?

David No.

Thomas (*almost a mutter*) Well, thank God for that. I know they *do* have
people. Where *do* you work?

David I'm at the International Stores.

Thomas Behind the counter—or what?

David Behind the counter.

Thomas What sort of wage do you get?

David Ten pounds a week.

Thomas (*amazed, and almost exasperated*) Ten . . . ? At your age? When
I was nineteen . . . You don't mean ten pounds clear, do you?

David (*shaking his head*) Less P.A.Y.E. and my insurance.

Thomas Even so . . . ! It's bloody—damn' good money. (*After a slight
pause*) Have you anything saved?

David A bit.

Thomas (*riled by David's reticence, but curbing his temper*) Mind telling
me how much?

David Just over a hundred pounds.

Thomas (*grudgingly*) H'm! Not bad! You're a better saver than I was at
your age. But perhaps I enjoyed life a bit more than you do. (*After a
slight pause*) Do you get out and about much?

David (*quietly, and not self-pityingly*) I—I haven't been out this last
month.

Thomas Why not?

David (*turning away, obviously distressed*) Mother was ill—in terrible pain—I spent all the time I could . . . (*He is near to tears*)

Thomas (*gruffly*) All right! All right! (*After a pause*) Got a girl?

David (*shaking his head*) No.

Thomas Not? Good Lord! At nineteen I had dozens. (*Looking towards him for a moment*) You like 'em, don't you?

David (*turning*) Like 'em?

Thomas Girls. You like their company?

David Yes, of course.

Thomas Well, it's time you got out and about among 'em—had some fun! God! I wish I could go back to your age again. I know . . . (*He pauses, then makes a fresh start*) Well now! What—plans—have you for your future? I mean—where do you intend to live now? Or haven't you got round to thinking about that yet? Obviously you'll have to leave here and . . .

There is a knock at the front door

Blast! You expectin' company?

David (*moving to the front door*) No. I don't know who . . . (*He opens the door*)

Major Webber is standing in the doorway. She wears Salvation Army uniform, and is a shortish pleasant-faced dumpling of a woman of fifty. She is wearing gold-rimmed spectacles

(*Seeing her; surprised*) Oh—Major . . . !

Thomas moves out of view of the doorway

Major (*in a subdued, but not sanctimonious voice*) Can I come in—just for a minute?

David (*after a quick look towards Thomas*) Of course.

Major (*as she comes in*) Thank you. I didn't get a chance to speak to you after the funeral. You were with . . . It *was* your father, wasn't it?

Thomas (*stepping forward; not aggressively*) That's right, ma'am.

Major (*turning*) Oh! (*Seeing Thomas*) I'm sorry! (*A little embarrassed*) I didn't realize . . . How do you do, Mr Armstrong?

David (*to Thomas*) Major Webber.

Thomas Major . . .? (*Then hurriedly*) Oh, yes, of course. Pleased to meet you, Major. (*He does not know whether he should shake hands or not*)

David Won't you sit down, Major?

Major But perhaps I'm interrupting—if you're discussing family matters . . .

Thomas (*not wildly enthusiastic*) No, no, that's all right.

David (*suddenly seeing the tea things*) Can I get you a cup of tea?

Major No thank you; I shall be having it when I get home.

David offers her a chair, and she sits. David goes to the table and puts the cup on the tray

David (*to Thomas*) Would you like another cup?

Thomas No.

David (*obviously ill at ease, speaking mostly to the Major*) Well—if you
don't mind I'll—I'll just get rid of the tray.

David takes the tray out through the kitchen door

Thomas (*after clearing his throat*) Were you wanting to talk to the lad
alone—er—Major?

Major No, no. It's just that—I saw you at the funeral with David, as I say,
but—(*hesitatingly*)—I didn't know whether you would—er—be here,
or not, and I couldn't bear to think of David being all on his own. If he
had been—I was going to ask him round to my place.

Thomas H'm! Very kind of you.

Major Not at all. I'm very fond of David. We all are—down at the
Citadel. He's—he's a good boy, Mr Armstrong.

Thomas H'm! Well that's nice to hear.

Major He was a great comfort to his mother, during her illness. He
devoted himself to her unsparingly. Not many sons of his age would
have done the same—not in these days, I'm afraid.

Thomas No, I suppose not.

Major (*after a slight pause*) Please don't think I'm—interfering, but I *am*
interested in his welfare. Er—what is going to happen to him now?
He'll be leaving here (*indicating the house*) of course, but is he going
to . . .?

Thomas As a matter of fact we were just getting round to that when you
knocked. It's something we've got to settle before I go back.

Major (*half rising*) Oh! Then perhaps I ought to leave you to . . .

David returns from the kitchen

Thomas (*half-heartedly*) No, no, don't go. You might . . . (*Seeing David*)
Ah there you are!

*Now the Major is present, Thomas is deliberately more cordial towards
David, but the cordiality must not be overdone*

Come and sit down, son. The—the Major was just asking me what your
future plans are, and I was saying that was the very thing we were going
to discuss when she knocked, weren't we? (*Again slightly irritable*) Sit
down, son, sit down. (*Then to the Major, as he lights a match*) You don't
mind the pipe—er—Major?

David sits by the table

Major No, no.

Thomas (*to David, lighting his pipe*) You don't smoke, son?

David (*quietly*) No.

Thomas You're very wise; expensive habit; wish I didn't. (*He blows out a
cloud of smoke. Briskly*) Now then! Do you want to stay on here—in
this town, I mean?

David (*somewhat surprised*) Yes, of course. I've got my job, and . . .

Thomas (*brusquely*) Plenty of jobs going if you did think of moving else-
where. Come to that, I daresay your firm'd give you a transfer. And it
might not be a bad idea to get right away from here, eh, Major!

Major (*doubtfully*) Well—er . . .

Thomas (*to David, sweeping on*) After all, you've lived here all your life, so far. No harm in—er—seeking 'fresh fields and pastures new', eh! I know if I was in your place and your age, this town wouldn't see me for dust! Nor this country, either. I'd be working my passage to somewhere just as soon as I could fix it up. (*After a slight pause*) But—(*with just a slight note of contempt*)—but travel doesn't appeal to you, eh?

David (*quietly*) I've never thought about it.

Thomas H'm! Well what . . . ? (*Not wildly enthusiastic*) Would you—would you think of coming to me at Nottingham? It's up to you; you can if you want to.

David (*after a look towards Thomas, lowering his eyes*) No, thanks. I want to stay here.

Thomas What do you say, Major?

Major (*a little embarrassed*) Since you ask me—and please don't be offended at what I am going to say—I don't think it would be very wise of David to come to you at Nottingham. I—(*almost murmuring*)—I do know how you are—placed there, and surely—David's being there would present problems?

Thomas (*with a somewhat sardonic grin*) Thank you, Major, for putting it so—tactfully, shall we say?

Major Oh, but I . . .

Thomas (*with a wave of the hand*) All right! All right! Let's forget the idea. The lad's obviously no more gone on it than you are. (*To David*) Well, I suppose it means—if you're going to stay here—you'll have to go into lodgings somewhere. Have you got anywhere in mind?

Major If you'd like to, David, you can come and stay with us for a while. My husband and I would be very glad to have you.

David It's very kind of you, but—I want to stay on here.

Thomas Stay where? (*Gulping*) You don't mean—here—in this house?

David Yes.

Major But, David . . . !

Thomas You mean—on your own? Looking after yourself?

David Yes.

Thomas Now don't be damn silly!

David (*quietly*) I've been looking after myself for the last month—while Mum was in hospital, haven't I, Major?

Major (*quickly*) Yes, Mr Armstrong, he has. (*To David*) But, David . . .

Thomas (*to David*) Look, son, I'm not saying you *couldn't* look after yourself—it's obvious (*with gesture indicating the room*) you *could*, but what sort of a life would it be for you? All work and no play at all. And you're at an age when you ought to be enjoying yourself—getting some fun out of life while you've the chance. I've told you that already.

Major You don't think a complete break from here—this house—might be better, David?

David I'll be all right, Major.

Major Well—if you think so. (*To Thomas*) Perhaps he should be allowed to give it a trial, Mr Armstrong—and if it doesn't work out . . .

Thomas (*almost surlily*) It isn't a question of his being 'allowed' to do any-thing. He's his own boss. I shan't interfere. But I only hope he realizes what he's letting himself in for, but it seems a mad idea to me. If he had a girl—and was engaged, and thinking of getting married within a few months, it'd be different, but . . . (*With a shrug*) Anyway, there it is! It's up to him. (*Suddenly*) By the way, do you know you *can* stay on here? The landlord mightn't want to let you—not on your own. And you're not the tenant; your mother was. He can turn you out if he wants to.

David (*quietly*) He'll let me stay.

Thomas (*with sharpness*) You mean you've seen him already?

David He came to see me yesterday.

Thomas (*growling*) Bit quick off the mark, wasn't he?

David He'd had one or two people making enquiries, so naturally . . .

Thomas But he's agreed to let you stay on.

David Yes. (*Quietly*) He said we'd always been good tenants, so . . .

Thomas Oh, well—that's that, I suppose. (*He moves away, dismissing the subject*)

There is a slight pause

Major (*rising and looking at her watch*) Well, if you will excuse me I think I ought to be . . .

Thomas (*a shade too quickly*) That's all right, Major, we mustn't keep you.

Major (*after a quiet smile*) I'm glad you're not going away and leaving us, David; so glad. I think that at a time like this you want to be amongst your friends—and here you know you *are* amongst them. I know you've been missed by all the young folk down at the Citadel these last few weeks. Well, now, I hope, in spite of all the work you'll have to do here —I hope you'll be able to get along there a bit more.

David (*with a smile*) I shall try.

Major (*indicating the cornet*) And don't neglect that, will you? You were getting along very nicely. (*With a little sigh and a smile*) Though how you're going to find time to do everything, I don't know.

David (*again the smile*) I will.

Major (*to Thomas*) Er—are you staying a day or two, Mr Armstrong?

Thomas No, I'm afraid not. I must get back to Nottingham tonight. Got to be at work at eight in the morning.

Major Come round to the house later this evening, if you wish. Don't decide now; see how you feel after your father has gone.

David Thank you, Major.

Major (*after a moment, putting a hand on his arm; quietly*) God be with you, David. (*After a slight pause*) Good-bye, Mr Armstrong.

Thomas Good-bye. (*Somewhat awkwardly*) Oh, and may I say I thought the—the service this afternoon was—was very impressive. And if you'd thank all your—er—colleagues for me—er—(*looking across at David*)— for *both* of us . . .

Major (*quietly*) I will. Thank you. (*She moves to the front door and looks out*) The rain seems to be stopping.

Thomas (*gruffly, and callously*) Well, thank God for that.

Major (*turning, with an impish smile on her face*) We *do*, Mr Armstrong. We thank God for *all* his blessings.

Thomas gapes at her

Major Webber exits to the street

Thomas closes the door and stands by it, lost in thought

Thomas (*gruffly*) H'm! Seems a nice enough woman, that.

David (*quietly*) She was wonderful while Mum was ill. Went up to see her at the hospital every day, without fail.

Thomas Not praying over her all the time, I hope!

David is silent.

Do you spent a lot of time down at this—Citadel place—I mean normally? These last few weeks, I know, you've had your time fully occupied—but . . .

David I go down quite a lot.

Thomas Week-nights as well as Sundays?

David There's something on most nights. I like to go when I can. We have a Youth Club, and . . .

Thomas They're not shovin' 'Blood and Fire' down your throat *all* the time, are they?

Again David is silent

(*Irritably*) Now don't get me wrong, but I had my basin full of religion with your mother. I don't understand it—especially the Salvation Army sort! All this 'washed in the Blood of Jesus'—I don't see where it gets you—except that it seems to land quite a few poor devils in the nut-house. And all this everlasting worryin' your inside out about the 'life hereafter'. I find it takes me all my time and energy coping with *this* one. (*More irritably*) But what's the use of talking? It's obvious they've got their claws into you, just as they had with your mother. (*After a slight pause*) Are you going round to—(*with jerk of head towards the front door*)—her place tonight?

David Well—what are you . . . ?

Thomas (*brusquely*) You don't have to bother about me. I'm going back to Nottingham—and you don't have to pretend to be disappointed. Have you got a time-table in the house—a railway time-table?

David No.

Thomas I ought to find out about trains. I forgot to ask at the station when I arrived. There's a telephone box at the end of the street if I remember rightly?

David Yes.

Thomas Yes, well—I'll go down there and ring up the station, then come back. I expect there are one or two things we ought to talk over yet. (*He moves to the door and opens it*)

David D'you want your mac?

Thomas No, it's fine now—(*with heavy sarcasm*)—praise be to God!

Thomas exits

David, left alone, stands quite still for a moment or two, then slowly and mechanically, begins to undo the buttons of his uniform jacket. He then looks slowly around the room, moves to the fireplace, then takes the photograph of himself and his mother from the mantelpiece, looks at it for a moment, then replaces it. He then notices the marriage certificate and letters which Thomas threw to the floor. He picks them up slowly, opens the certificate and looks at it. He then puts it—and the letters—in a drawer in the dresser. He moves down to the table, picks up the cornet and makes to put it in the box, hesitates, runs his hand over it, then crosses and sits on the lower fender seat, and after hesitating for a moment, puts the cornet to his lips and very quietly, and not too expertly, begins to play the hymn: 'There is a Green Hill Far Away.' As he reaches the end of the verse—

the CURTAIN falls

SCENE 2

The same. Evening, a month later.

When the CURTAIN rises, David is discovered seated at the table, which is laid for tea—quite neatly so, with a small, clean tablecloth and in the centre of the table a small bowl with artificial flowers—primroses, crocuses, etc. The table—without being fussy—looks 'appetizing'—and one might be surprised to learn—if one did not already know—that it is laid by, and for, a youth of nineteen, living alone. The entire room looks as neat as ever.

David is just finishing his 'main course'—scrambled egg on toast. He does this leisurely, then having finished the egg, he lays his knife and fork neatly side by side on the plate, and takes the plate out into the kitchen.

He returns, moves to the mantelpiece, takes down two unopened letters which are propped against an ornament, returns to the table, drinks from his tea-cup, pours out another cup, cuts himself a slice of cake from a small cake which is on a plate and doyley. He takes a bite of his cake, and opens the letters in turn and reads them. The first letter he opens is obviously the 'rates'. David looks at it for a moment, and gives a low whistle—half surprise, half dismay. He then moves to the dresser, and from one of the cupboards produces a file—the wooden base with a long spike type—on which are skewered quite a number of bills. Without removing them, he searches down through several bills until he finds the one he is looking for. Again, without removing it, he compares the bill on the file with the one he is holding in his hand. After a moment he gives a shrug of the shoulders, returns the file to the cupboard and sits at the table again—drinks some tea, and eats some cake. He then opens the second letter—also a bill. For a moment or two he looks at it, then lays it slowly down by the other one on the table, sits quite still for a moment, then, deliberately pulling himself together, drinks

13

*some more tea. There is a knock at the front door. David puts the cup down,
rises and crosses to the door and opens it.*

> *Bess Jones is on the doorstep. Bess is between thirty and thirty-five years
> of age, a little too plump perhaps, though not fat—yet. She is working-
> class and radiates cheerfulness and warmth. Her accent is North Country*

Bess (*brightly*) 'Evenin'.
David Good evening.
Bess Er—is your mother in?
David My . . . ?
Bess Well—Mrs Armstrong.
David (*confused*) Er—my mother—she isn't—she . . .
Bess (*suddenly doubtful*) This is number *thirty-two* Beaconsfield Road,
isn't it? Don't say I've come to the wrong house.
David Yes, this is number thirty-two, but . . .
Bess I thought I hadn't got it wrong. Well, you see . . . (*Breaking off*)
Look, love, d'you mind if I step inside a minute. (*With a shiver*) It's a
bit parky out here.

David hesitates for a second

> (*With a big smile*) I won't gollop you up—I promise!

David smiles back and stands aside for her to come in

David (*murmuring*) Please—come in.

Bess comes into the room. She is wearing a warm coat and a headscarf

Bess Ta, love. (*At once*) Ooh! Isn't it lovely and warm in here. (*Looking
round, automatically*) Well, what I've come about . . . (*Seeing the table
laid*) Oh dear! Don't say I've butted in right when you're havin' your
tea.
David (*hastily*) No, no. I'd just finished.
Bess (*smiling*) You little fibber, you hadn't!

David looks at her somewhat surprised

> (*Pointing*) You've half a cup of tea left yet. And what about all that
> cake on your plate?

David smiles

> (*Smiling back*) Sherlock Holmes, love, that's me. Go on, now; sit down
> and finish. Nothing I hate more than half-cold tea. (*After a slight pause*)
> Nothing I like more than a nice cup of *hot*!

David (*Bess is sweeping him off his feet*) Oh! Well—er—this (*putting his
hand round the teapot*) is still hot if . . .
Bess (*smiling and with obviously false protestation*) Oh, love, you *didn't*
think I was hinting, did you?
David (*smiling*) Yes.
Bess Well, you were right; I was.
David I'll get another cup. Won't be a second. Sit down, won't you?

David goes into the kitchen

14

Bess (*as he is going; genuinely*) Oooh, you are kind!

Bess undoes her headscarf and lets it fall over her shoulders. She also un-buttons her coat and sits, looking around the room. She puts her handbag by the side of her chair

David returns with a cup and saucer

(*Cheerfully*) I say! I feel ever so guilty—practically forcing you to . . . I hope it's all right. I mean I hope your mother—or whatever Mrs Armstrong is to you, won't mind. Isn't she in?

David (*pulled up for a moment*) There—there isn't a Mrs Armstrong. (*Then very quickly*) D'you take sugar?

Bess Well I *don't*—but I *do*—but I *shouldn't*.

David looks at her

(*Smiling*) I'm tryin' ever so not very hard to lose a bit of weight. One lump, please. And for Gawd's sake don't ask me to have a piece of cake!

David brings tea to her

Ta! Now you sit down and finish your own.

David sits at the table and during the following dialogue finishes his tea

(*After taking a drink*) Ooh! That was good. (*Practically*) Look, what I've really come about is that advert in Johnson's showcase in the High Road—Johnson's the newsagents and tobacconists. Do *you* know any-thing about it—the advert I mean?

David almost gapes at Bess

David (*blankly*) *You've* come about . . . But it says on the card . . .

Bess Oh, you *do* know! (*Quickly*) I know what it says, love! It says 'Single room vacant, suitable for young man'.

David Yes. Well . . . !

Bess But that's nothing to go by—not really. It nearly always *does* say 'suitable for young man'. And when you've lived in digs as long as I have, and you see an advert that says 'suitable for young lady', you keep as far away as possible!

David suddenly laughs

What are you laughing at?

David You!

Bess (*blankly*) Come again!

David *I* put that advert in Johnson's.

Bess (*puzzled*) How d'you mean—*you* put it in?

David It's me that's letting a room.

Bess (*puzzled*) Look, love, I don't get this. (*Pointing to him*) *You* are letting a room?

David Yes.

Bess You mean this is—your house?

David I pay the rent.

Bess But you don't look old enough to be running a house.

15

David Well, I do.

Bess Good Lord! You're *not* married, are you?

David No.

Bess How old are you then?

David Nineteen.

Bess But what about your people—your parents?

David My mother died a month ago.

Bess I am sorry. (*Quietly*) And what about your father? Is he . . . ?

David (*moving away; quietly*) He lives at Nottingham.

Bess He works there, eh? But I suppose he . . .

David (*quietly but firmly*) He lives there.

Bess (*embarrassed*) Oh! (*After a slight pause*) And haven't you no sisters or brothers?

David No.

Bess (*quietly*) Oh dear! You are on your lonesome, aren't you? (*After a slight pause*) Then—who looks after you here?

David I look after myself.

Bess No, I mean—who cleans the place? You must have somebody to help you.

David (*shaking his head*) I do it myself.

Bess (*surprised*) Go on! You never do!

David Honest.

Bess And do you go out to work as well?

David Huh-huh!

Bess Well, by heck! I'd never've believed . . . I mean—a lad of your age! But don't you find it lonely?

David (*after a pause; quietly*) A bit I do, yes.

Bess (*after a look at him*) You mean a *lot* you do, don't you?

Note: It is important that from the moment Bess learns that David is alone in the house, she shows no desire to stay in it. The thought never enters her head, and throughout the scene her attitude to David is never anything but sympathetic friendliness

David Sometimes. (*With a shrug*) But I'm at work all day—I don't come home for my dinner; I get it out.

Bess And when do you do your—your housework?

David (*with a smile*) I ought to be doing it now.

Bess Is that a hint for me to be gettin' my skates on? (*She automatically picks up her handbag*)

David (*quickly*) No, no, of course not. Don't go yet—unless you've got to go and see some other rooms.

Bess (*replacing her handbag*) Well, I've got to find *somewhere*. I mean I've drawn a blank here, haven't I? Can't get round the 'suitable for young man' this time.

David D'you mean you've nowhere to stay tonight?

Bess No, I haven't. I'm in a proper pickle! My landlady's had to rush off this afternoon to (*Using a 'cod' Welsh accent*) Cardiff, look you! To nurse an old uncle with lots and lots of money, indeed to goodness.

16

(*Dropping the accent*) She may be away weeks and she wasn't at all keen on leaving me alone in the house with her husband, though the Lord knows what she's worrying about. The poor devil can hardly get across the room on a couple of sticks, so what she imagines we were going to get up to, both of us . . . !

She looks towards David, who is looking rather embarrassed by all this—but his face breaks into a smile

(*Going on quickly*) Anyway, that's neither here not there. The point is I've got to find a room right away.
David (*murmuring*) Oh dear!
Bess (*brightly*) Oh, I'll find somewhere, don't worry. And if I don't, I can go and stay in a hotel just for one night. (*With a smile*) My name's Rothschild—didn't you know?
David What *is* your name?
Bess Elizabeth—Elizabeth Jones, but life being so short and everybody in such a tearin' hurry to get through it—I usually get 'Bess'.
David Are you—er—married?
Bess No, why? Are you going to propose to me?

David laughs

Y'know you don't look a day over seven when you laugh. If I were you I should make a habit of it, it suits you. What's your *christian* name?
David David.
Bess H'm! Nice! (*With a smile*) Pleased to meet you—David.
David Thanks. Same here—Bess.
Bess (*with a grin*) Oh! You cheeky young thing, you!

There follows a silence. For once, even Bess cannot think of anything to say. She is very conscious of David looking at her—he is captivated by her warmth and brightness

David (*at length*) Er—would you like another cup of tea? It won't take me a minute to make some fresh.
Bess No thanks, love—(*handing her cup and saucer to him*)—but that was lovely. Just what I needed.

David takes the cup and saucer to the table

Are you going to wash up now? Can I give you a hand? (*She rises and moves towards the table*)
David No, thanks. It can wait. You're North Country, aren't you?
Bess (*with a grin*) Ee' ba goom, I am an' all! Lancashire; the real genuine article; born in Blackpool, love. Couldn't be more genuine than that, could I? (*She looks, almost unconsciously, at the table while talking. In surprise*) I say!
David What? (*He makes as if to start clearing the table*)
Bess (*putting out a hand to stop him; still with surprise in her voice*) No, just a minute! Don't touch it!
David (*puzzled*) What?

17

Bess I'm just looking at your tea-table; thinking how nice it looks. Did you set it? (*Quickly*) Well, of course you must've done; silly of me to ask, but—it's set so—so nicely—nice clean cloth—and everything laid out so—so—neatly—what you might call appetizing. I do try very hard to be tidy, but . . . ! But you take the biscuit, you do. (*Turning*) Your mother's brought you up well—that's obvious.

David stiffens for a moment

(*Noticing this; quickly*) I'm sorry, love. I shouldn't've . . . (*Quietly*) You miss her badly, don't you?

David I forget—sometimes—for a bit, then . . . (*Moving to the fireplace and picking up the photograph*) I've got a photograph of her here, if you'd like to see it.

Bess (*genuinely*) Oh, I would—yes. But I don't want you to upset yourself now.

David (*coming to her; after a smile at her*) It's both of us, actually. We had it taken about a year ago. (*He hands the photograph to Bess*)

Bess (*almost at once; as she looks at the photograph*) Oh yes! It's good to tell you're mother and son. Aren't you like her? And—(*she stops and almost peers at the photograph*)—why—what's the . . . ? (*Looking at David; obviously puzzled*) Is this Salvation Army uniform you're both wearing?

David That's right.

Bess You mean—you belong to the Salvation Army?

David Yes.

Bess (*somewhat nonplussed*) Well—fancy! (*She is embarrassed for a moment. Looking at the photograph again*) Well, I must say, the uniform suits you.

David (*smiling*) Thanks.

Bess Or is it you that suits the uniform? (*She looks at the photograph again, then begins to laugh quietly*)

David (*puzzled*) What . . . ?

Bess Oh, nothing, love. I was just remembering—I wore Salvation Army uniform once. Oo! I must've looked a duck!

David *You* did?

Bess (*smiling at him*) Huh-huh! Just after I left school. I went to work at St Annes-on-sea—that's near Blackpool—and I had a bit of a voice like, so I joined the local Operatic Society, and we did *The Belle of New York* one time, God forgive us!—and I played 'The Belle'—and that's more than *anybody* could forgive!

David (*puzzled*) 'The Belle' . . . ?

Bess Oo! Aren't you ignorant. 'The Belle of New York'—she's a Salvation Army lass—and she converts everybody in three acts. (*Suddenly singing and giving an exaggerated imitation of the demure 'Belle'*)

> They never seem to follow that light
> They only—follow—*me*!

They both laugh heartily, then as Bess's eyes fall on the photograph which

18

she is still holding, she sobers up. David's eyes have followed hers to the photograph; he too becomes serious again

(*After a moment, handing him the photograph*) P'raps you'd better . . .

David takes the photograph from her, and looking at it, moves up to the mantelpiece, and replaces it

(*Soberly*) You're not cross with me?

David turns and looks at her quizzically

I wasn't taking the mickey out of the Salvation Army, honest I wasn't. I know they're really wonderful people—wonderful! *The things they do!* (*Quite seriously*) I remember my dad saying—when he was in the R.A.F. he *always* used the Salvation Army canteen if he could 'cos they put twice as much meat in their sausages as the Y.M.C.A. (*She moves to the table*)

David looks at her blankly for a moment, then bursts out laughing again, moving away

(*Innocently*) Oo! Have I said something? (*She picks up a knife and cuts a small piece of cake. With a smile*) You're not looking, are you?

David turns

(*Holding up the cake*) The spirit is strong, but you've no idea how weak the flesh is. (*She takes a bite of cake*)

David (*eagerly*) Look! Why don't you let me get you a proper tea? It won't take long.

Bess 'Get thee behind me, Satan!' No, it's very kind of you, love, but— I'll have to be going.

David (*innocently, eagerly*) Oh, but do you have to? I mean you're not in *my* way.

Bess (*mock 'hoity-toity'*) Thanks very much!

David (*laughing*) I didn't mean that. What I meant was—well it's been ever so nice . . . (*His voice has tailed away*)

He stands, looking at Bess for a moment, then lowers his eyes. He is obviously embarrassed

Bess (*quietly*) You oughtn't to be living here on your own, you know. It can't be good for you.

David (*nodding his head; quietly*) I know. I *do* realize that. That's why I put that card in Johnson's.

Bess When did you put it in? I only happened to see it when I was passing this morning.

David Two days ago.

Bess Have you had anybody else call round besides me?

David Yes. Last night a young chap came. I showed him the room and he said he liked it and he'd come back and let me know definite in an hour's time—but he didn't.

Bess (*murmuring sympathetically*) Yes, you'll get a lot of them! Nosey parkers—that's all they are.

David Oh, I think he really was thinking of moving in, but . . .

19

Bess But what?

David Well—he happened to see my Salvation Army cap—it was hanging behind the door, and I think it—sort of—scared him off.

Bess (*with a rueful smile*) P'raps he thought you'd be banging a tambourine all night. (*Looking towards the door*) Your cap isn't behind the door now.

David (*with a half smile*) No.

Bess (*smiling*) Artful, aren't you? (*There is a slight pause*) Isn't there anyone down at your—what d'you call the place where you have your meetings—er . . . ?

David The Citadel?

Bess That's right. Isn't there anyone there who'd come to share with you?

David (*not mournfully*) No, as it happens. All the young fellows seem to have their homes.

Bess (*suddenly*) Look! Would you mind if I had a *look* at the room?

David (*surprised*) Why . . . ?

Bess (*quickly*) Oh, don't think I'm getting ideas. It's not for myself, but—I *might* be able to do something. We *do* get quite a lot of young chaps in our place—really nice, some of 'em, and—well, you never know, do you? And if I'm going to recommend something, I ought to know what I'm recommending, oughtn't I?

David You mean—where you work you get young chaps in?

Bess (*suddenly a bit embarrassed*) Yes.

David Where's that?

Bess (*with a half smile*) I think I'd better open the front door before I tell you—so as I can make a bolt for it.

David Why?

Bess (*after a slight pause*) I'm a barmaid at the *Golden Lion*.

David (*very serious and perturbed*) Oh!

Bess Yes—(*imitating him*)—'Oh!' You people don't believe in—*Golden Lions*, do you?

David No.

Bess No, I know you don't. (*Pointedly, but without malice*) Except on Saturday nights when you want to sell your *War Cry*'s (*She smiles at him*) Don't look so serious! I haven't got a bottle of gin in my handbag.

David Er—do you drink?

Bess I—I have been known to.

David (*as before*) Oh!

Bess Yes, and now I suppose you're picturing me careering round the tap room with my skirt up over my thighs, singing *Knees Up Mother Brown*!

David (*laughing in spite of himself*) You are daft!

Bess (*with mock severity*) Hey! Are them the sort of manners they teach you in the 'Sally's Army'? Talking to a lady like that, and I'm older than you, don't forget.

David is about to speak

20

(*Quickly*) And don't ask me how old I *am*, 'cos I shan't tell you. (*After a slight pause*) Well, what about it?

David What about what?

Bess This famous room—am I going to see it, or aren't I?

David Well—er—yes—if you . . . It's—it's upstairs.

Bess You surprise me!

David Er—shall I come up with you?

Bess (*muttering under her breath*) Oh my God—(*quickly*)—fathers! Of course you'll come with me. But if it'll make you feel safer, you'd better bring the bread knife with you—in *case* I start getting fresh! Come on!

David moves to the staircase door and opens it, revealing the narrow turn of stairs

(*Looking at the stairs*) These stairs are a bit antiquated, aren't they?

David These are old-fashioned houses.

Bess You're telling me! (*She goes up a step then turns*) Er—just a minute!

David What?

Bess Excuse me asking but is the—er—'what's it' up here?

David The . . . ?

Bess (*patiently*) The toilet, love.

David (*confused*) Oh—er—yes. It's—er—in the bathroom, first door on the right.

Bess Yes, quite. Well—would you mind just giving me half a minute.

David (*more confused*) Oh—er . . .

Bess The call of nature, love. I know it's indelicate to mention it, but needs must when the devil drives—and I'm not going to bust my bladder for anybody. Won't be a tick!

Bess exits up the stairs

David stands for a moment somewhat bewildered. Then he smiles to himself, half-closes the staircase door and moves absently over to the table and begins —almost automatically—to collect the tea things together but his mind is not fully on what he is doing. There is a knock at the front door. David, who has one or two crocks in his hands, gives a start, and just manages to save the crocks from falling. He puts them down on the table, hesitates—looks towards the stairs, rather panicky. After a moment he goes and quietly closes and latches the staircase door, then, after another moment of hesitation, moves to the front door. Before he can reach it, the knocking is heard again. He waits until the knocking has stopped, then opens the door

Major Webber is standing on the doorstep. She is in her uniform

Seeing the Major, David gives another guilty little start

David (*with a gasp of surprise*) Major!

Major Good evening, David.

David Good . . . (*He stands nonplussed for a moment*)

Major (*after a slight pause*) Er—may I come in?

David (*vaguely*) What? (*Then pulling himself together*) Oh yes, of course, Major; I'm sorry. Please. (*He stands aside to let her pass*)

The Major enters. When she has passed David, he gives a quick anxious look towards the stairs

Major (*smiling and speaking quizzically*) You weren't asleep, were you?
David (*blinking*) Asleep?
Major (*laughing*) I believe you were. In fact I don't think you're thoroughly awake yet! You look quite dazed!
David Do I? Well—I wasn't asleep, Major. I was just going to wash up. I . . . (*He looks towards the table and notices the two cups and saucers. He gives a little start then turns quickly to the Major*) Oh—(*indicating the sofa*)—er—do sit down, Major!
Major Thank you.

While the Major is moving to the sofa, David quickly whips the tea-cosy off the teapot and puts it over one cup and saucer

(*As she sits*) Though I can't stay long. I have a meeting shortly. I mustn't be late. But I wanted to see you this evening.
David (*trying not to look towards the staircase door*) Why—what . . . ?
Major (*smiling at him*) Oh, it's nothing terrible. I haven't come to lecture you. No, it's simply this. You told me the other day—remember—that you had definitely decided to let one of your rooms—if you could find a suitable tenant.
David Oh—er—yes, Major.
Major Have you let it yet?
David (*still distrait*) No—no I haven't actually. I've put a card in a shop showcase. Somebody told me that was the best thing to do.
Major But you haven't let it to anyone?
David No.
Major I'm so glad, because I've found—at least I hope I've found—someone who might be ideal.
David Oh?
Major Yes. He's a young man who has come to work here in the town—at Boots the Chemists. He only arrived last week. He's from London. He's in rooms in Western Road—he took them for a week on trial, but he's not very happy there and wants to get out on Saturday if he can.
David (*only half listening*) Oh! Er—is he a Salvationist?
Major No. He's a Catholic. (*With a smile*) But we won't hold that against him, will we?
David Of course not.
Major Well this afternoon . . . (*She suddenly breaks off*) What was that?
David What?
Major I thought I heard footsteps. (*She looks towards the ceiling; then continues imperturbedly*) Must have been next door. Er—where was I? Oh yes! I was in Boots this afternoon and this young man happened to serve me. I explained that if he did come here he'd have to look after himself quite a lot. He didn't seem to mind; said he'd prefer it. He seems quite nice, David. Nice and quiet.
David H'm.

22

Major His name is Watson—John Watson. Can I ask him to come round and see you?

David Er . . . yes. (*Moving to the fireplace and standing with his back half-turned from the Major*) Yes, of course.

Major (*rising*) Good! He could come round tomorrow evening as soon as he leaves work, if that's convenient.

David (*vaguely*) Tomorrow . . . ?

Major (*moving near the chair Bess was sitting in*) Actually, he wanted to come round tonight, but I told him there was no point in him doing that—that you'd most probably let the room by now, but I promised to find out and . . . (*She sees Bess's handbag beside the chair. Her voice tails away, and she looks at the bag in silence. She does not give a violent start on seeing it, nor does she suspect 'the worst', although—remembering—her eyes do go up to the ceiling for a moment. She looks towards David somewhat baffled*)

David is turned towards the fireplace, wrapped in his own thoughts

Er—David . . . ?

David (*turning*) Yes?

The Major is about to speak of the bag, but suddenly decides not to do so

Major Shall I tell Mr Watson to come round tomorrow evening, then?

David (*not too eagerly*) Yes, yes, of course. (*After a slight pause*) Thank you for thinking of it, Major.

Major (*quietly*) I'm only too glad to be able to help—both of you.

David gives a little smile

Well, I must be going.

David moves almost too quickly up to the door, and half opens it. The Major is aware of the quick move. Again she is baffled. She moves slowly up to the door

(*Stopping by David*) By the way—er—what are you asking for the room?

David Well—two pounds a week—that's what I've put on the card.

Major That seems very reasonable. I'll tell him.

David Thank you, Major.

Major And when are we going to see you at the Citadel again—during the week, I mean?

David (*smiling*) Very soon now, I hope. But there *has* been a lot to see to.

Major (*nodding*) I know. Have you—have you heard from your father since he went back to Nottingham?

David (*quietly*) No. We don't write to each other.

Major I see. (*More brightly*) Well, good-bye for now, David. (*She puts a hand on his arm*) I hope you do decide to let Mr Watson have the room. I'm sure he'll be good company for you. And you need someone here, David. I'm certain it isn't good for you, being on your own.

David gives another little smile

(*Quietly*) God bless you, David. Good-bye.

David Good-bye, Major—and thank you again.

The Major, after a warm smile, departs

David, after closing the door, moves slowly to the fireplace—one hand smoothing his hair down, absently. He stands facing the fire. There is a pause

> *Then the staircase door opens slowly and Bess's head comes cautiously round it. She gives an exaggerated look round the room, then looks towards David*

Bess (*with only her head showing*) Ahem!

David spins around.

David Oh!

Bess (*sweetly*) The name is Jones. Miss Elizabeth Jones. Remember me?

David (*laughing*) I'm *sorry*, but—just for a moment, I . . .

Bess (*opening the door wider*) You'd forgotten me. (*Putting it into quotes*) You don't have to tell me; I know!

David I hadn't really forgotten. In fact I've been anxious about you.

Bess (*smiling*) I'll bet you have! Bit tricky, that, wasn't it?

David What?

Bess You know very well what; me being up there. (*She points*)

David (*with bravado*) Oh, I don't know!

Bess Now come off it! I'll *bet* you were scared stiff I'd come marching down those stairs at any minute.

David (*smiling*) We don't bet; we don't believe in it.

Bess (*smiling*) And don't be so smug! Anyway you didn't tell her you'd— you'd got a woman upstairs, did you? Be honest.

David (*grinning*) No. And how d'you know it was a 'her'?

Bess I peeped out of the bedroom window when she went. Who was she?

David She's from the Citadel—she belongs to the Salvation Army too.

Bess Look! I'm not blind—I didn't think she was in the Folies Bergère. She looked a real homely body. Kind an' nice.

David She is—very nice; very understanding.

Bess (*with a little laugh*) I wonder how 'understanding' she'd have been if she'd known I was upstairs.

Bess stands for a moment in thought. Then little quiet bursts of laughter come from her. The laughter increases until she is laughing heartily. She moves to her bag, picks it up and extracts a handkerchief. David, watching her, finds himself joining in the laughter

> (*Becoming aware of this—between the laughs—wiping her eyes*) What are *you* laughing at?

David (*laughing*) I—I don't know! What are you?

Bess I was thinking of myself—just now—(*she laughs*)—up in your—er— bathroom—not knowing whether I dare come out or not—(*more laughter*)—in case—whoever it was—heard me. I—I—just sat there— on the seat—(*she is convulsed*)—I—I didn't even dare pull the chain! (*She yelps with laughter*)

David tries, unsuccessfully, to be horrified, but it is a hopeless attempt. He gives himself up to unrestrained laughter

(*She pulls herself together for a moment*) Oh, stop it, for goodness' sake!

David, gradually, stops laughing. They look at each other for a moment, then simultaneously burst out again

(*At last, almost groaning*) Oh, do pull yourself together! (*She takes a compact from her bag, opens it and looks at herself in the lid mirror. Her voice is still trembling with laughter*) Just look at my face! Looks like a lump of cat meat! (*She does a speedy repair job on her face, then puts the compact away*) Now come on! (*Looking away from David*) Let's be sensible. I'll have to go in a minute.

David is pulled up with a jerk. All trace of laughter leaves his face immediately

David Oh, but . . .
Bess I've seen the room. It's the front one, isn't it?
David (*quietly*) Yes.
Bess I thought so. I peeped in all three actually. Hope you don't mind?
David (*as before*) No, of course not.
Bess A very nice room, that front one.
David (*quieter still*) It was Mum's. (*He half turns away*)

Bess looks at him quickly for a moment as if about to say something, but changes her mind

Bess (*with deliberate practicality*) Very nice. You needn't mind offering that to anyone. If you'd seen some of the bedrooms I've had . . . ! (*Preparing to depart*) Well—if I *do* hear of anyone, would you like me to send 'em along? I'd make pretty sure they were all right before I did, of course. What do you say?
David (*not enthusiastically*) Well as a matter of fact—Major Webber . . .
Bess Major Webber?
David The person who called just now. That's *why* she called really—to say there's a young fellow she knows who, she's pretty certain, would take the room. He's calling round tomorrow night.
Bess (*pleased, brightly*) Oh, well, that's that, isn't it! Couldn't be better.

David turns to the fireplace

(*Still quite brightly*) Well—I'll be on my travels.

David spins round

(*Busy putting on her headscarf*) Thanks ever so much, love, for the tea and—everything. And—we've had a good laugh, haven't we? And I hope everything turns out right—with this young fellow who's coming to see the room, I mean. And p'raps I'll see you one Sunday when you're out with the Salvation Army. If I do I'll give you a wave—just a little private one—you know—(*she demonstrates the wave*)—I won't embarrass you. (*Satisfied that she is ready for departure*) Right then! (*She moves to the door*)

25

The sound of a train rushing by is heard. David watches Bess from the fire-place. He cannot move. As Bess begins to open the door he is jerked into desperation

David (*quite loudly; half a shout, half an agonized appeal*) Bess!

Bess spins round, quite startled.

Bess What? What on earth . . . ?

David, unable to speak, almost stumbles across to near her, shaking his head violently

(*Alarmed for him*) 'Ee, love, what's the matter?

David pushes the door closed with one hand

David No!

Bess (*bewildered*) Hey . . . !

David (*desperately*) Please—don't go!

Bess (*as before*) What?

David I mean—won't you come to stay? *You* take the room—*please!*

Bess (*staggered*) *What?*

David *Please!*

Bess But . . . (*She is quite genuinely amazed at David's suggestion*)

David *Please!*

Bess Now, look . . . !

David (*desperately*) You've just said what a nice room it is, so why don't you take it. *Please!*

Bess (*not unkindly*) It's—kind of you to suggest it, but . . .

David I'm *not* being kind. I *want* you to take it. It would be wonderful having you here. You're so—so—happy and . . . Please, Bess!

Bess Now listen! You're just being silly. You know it wouldn't do at all, for me to stay here alone with you. (*Quickly*) Oh I know I'm nearly old enough to be your mother, but what are people going to say? No, love, you can forget the idea.

David Nobody'll say anything, and anyway we'll know there's nothing—nothing wrong. And I'll tell everybody what a wonderful person you are.

Bess (*pleased, but protesting*) Oh, love . . .

David (*overlapping*) I'll tell them how you make me laugh. I—I haven't laughed, Bess, not for a long time—not like we did just now. I'll tell them I begged you to stay. (*Desperately*) Please, Bess . . .

Bess (*beginning to weaken for the first time*) It's—it's just plain silly.

David I do want you to stay. I can't tell you how much. I'll see to every-thing. I'll look after you.

Bess (*with a little laugh*) *You'll* look after *me*?

David (*more desperately*) You know what I . . . Bess, will you? Will you?

Bess (*obviously giving in*) It's ridiculous. Damned ridiculous.

David It isn't, Bess, it isn't. I'm certain you were *meant* to come here.

Bess 'Meant to'? What on earth are you talking about?

David (*embarrassed*) I—I can't explain. But, *please* say you'll stay.

Bess Now look, love . . .

26

David Bess—please!

There is quite a long pause. Bess, obviously far from happy at the idea, stands looking worried. She is not looking at David, but three times she glances at him, then away again, before coming to a decision. David never takes his eyes off her

Bess (*with a doubtful sigh*) All right, then.

David (*almost wildly*) You *will*?

Bess If—you're sure . . .

David Oh, *Bess!* (*His arms go round her and he hugs her closely. His cheek is next to hers. He does not kiss her*)

Bess (*when she can speak*) Thank you very much! That's *quite* enough of that! (*She disengages herself firmly*)

David (*flustered*) I'm sorry. I didn't mean . . .

Bess (*with mock severity*) I hope you weren't starting the way you mean to go on!

David (*still flustered*) No—no. Oh, Bess, I'm so glad you . . .

Bess (*very practically, waving a hand to silence him*) All right! All right! 'Nuff said! Well—I suppose I'd better go and collect my belongings. I took 'em along to the *Golden Lion* at lunch time. I'll just have time to bring them here before I go back on duty. (*She consults her watch*)

David (*eagerly*) Shall I come with you? Help you carry them?

Bess (*firmly*) No you won't! That'd be a good kick-off, wouldn't it, if some of your Salvation Army pals saw you hanging round the *Golden Lion* waiting for a barmaid! I'll go myself. (*She turns to open the door*)

David (*suddenly, anxiously*) Bess!

Bess (*turning; patiently*) *Now* what?

David You—you do mean it? You *will*—come back?

Bess (*almost as if she doubted it herself*) I'll be back.

David (*desperately urgent*) Honest?

Bess hesitates for a fraction of a second, looks at David's anxious face, smiles, then suddenly puts out a hand and ruffles his hair

Bess (*quietly but firmly*) I'll be back!

As she turns and opens the door, with David watching her—

the CURTAIN *falls*

27

ACT II

SCENE 1

The same. Evening, three weeks later.

The table is laid for a meal for two—not so meticulously as in the last scene. The bowl of artificial flowers is on the dresser. The room is not wildly untidy, but there are a few things lying around. For instance, on one chair there is an opened and rather crumpled women's magazine; on the arm of the chair is an opened packet of cigarettes and a lighter. Bess's coat is also on a chair. A cushion has fallen from the sofa to the floor.

When the CURTAIN *rises, Bess, in jumper and skirt, is by the fireplace 'doing' her face; she applies powder and lipstick quite moderately. Having finished and patted her hair as she looks in the mirror over the mantelpiece, she compares the time by her watch with the clock on the mantelpiece, then winds the watch. She then moves to the paper-rack beside the fire, takes out a morning paper, notices another paper in the rack, takes it out. It is the 'War Cry'. She looks at it rather as she would look at a snake and, still standing by the fire, turns the pages over almost gingerly.*

Bess (*just audibly, as she looks at 'War Cry'*) Oh my Gawd! (*Deciding very firmly that it is not for her she puts 'War Cry' back in the rack. Then, after looking round the room, she begins to sing, very quietly, to herself, opening the morning paper while she does so*)

> 'She is the Belle of New York.
> The subject of all the town talk.
> She makes the whole Bowery
> Fragrant and flowery . . .'

As her interest in the paper develops, her singing tails away. She sits in the armchair reading

After a moment or two, the front door opens quickly and David bursts into the room. He is wearing a mackintosh, but no hat. He is now much happier and livelier than in the previous act. The moment he comes in he looks quickly round

David (*seeing Bess; brightly*) Hullo!
Bess (*looking up and smiling*) Hullo!

David comes down to near Bess's chair and just stands looking at her—happily

(*Aware of this*) It is me. And I'm still here.

David continues to look at Bess happily for a moment, as if convincing himself that she is still here, then takes off his mac, hangs it up behind the door, takes a twenty packet of cigarettes from one of the pockets and brings it down to Bess

28

David (*holding out the packet*) For you.

Bess (*protesting*) Oh, now—look . . . !

David (*smiling*) It's pay day.

Bess (*taking the packet*) It was pay day last week when I told you you weren't to do this any more—chucking your money about.

David But I like to do it. 'Sides—(*without any sadness*)—I always used to bring Mum some chocolates or something on Fridays, after I was paid. It's a habit I've got into.

Bess Well, thank you, love, but I'm not your mum, and these aren't chocolates. And what's more, you don't really approve of me smoking, do you—well, not in the house anyway.

David (*laughing*) Don't be daft. You know you can smoke as much as you like. (*Moving to the table*) Is the kettle on?

Bess (*rising*) Oh! Hope it isn't boiled dry. I forgot—damn!

David (*quickly putting her back into the chair; quite happily*) Don't worry. I'll see to it. (*He moves to the kitchen door, then turns and grins at her*)

David goes into the kitchen

Left alone, Bess looks at the packet of cigarettes in her hand, turning them over as she does so. Her expression suggests that she is rather worried. After a moment she shrugs her shoulders and puts the cigarettes down on a small table

David returns from the kitchen

Bess I opened that tin of salmon you left out—was that right?

David Yes. That's fine.

Bess And I cut the bread and butter.

David Yes. I saw that. And thanks for laying the table. (*He moves to it, his eyes go over it quickly as he speaks*) I like these Fridays when it's your day off and we can have tea together. (*He automatically begins to alter things on the table to his own satisfaction*)

Bess watches him doing this. David moves up to the dresser, takes the bowl of flowers and puts it in the centre of the table.

Bess (*smiling*) Shouldn't they be about half an inch to the left?

David H'mm?

Bess The flowers. I'm sure they're not dead centre.

David (*looking quickly at the flowers, then at Bess*) Gertcher! (*He now moves around smartly, tidying up the room—folding papers, etc. He does this quite automatically*) Been out this afternoon? (*He hangs Bess's coat behind the door*)

Bess Huh-huh! (*She watches the clearing-up operation*)

David Where did you go?

Bess (*after a slight pause*) The pictures.

David (*looking somewhat surprised*) The pictures?

Bess Yes. That new Richard Burton film at the A.B.C.

David (*perturbed*) Oh, but—I thought . . .

Bess What did you think? (*She watches him*)

David (*with a shrug*) Oh, never mind. (*He puts the cigarette packet and lighter from the chair on to a side table*)

 David turns from the side table, sees Bess looking towards him, gives her a smile, then goes into the kitchen

Bess moves to the table and stands looking at it

 David returns from the kitchen carrying a dish with tinned salmon on it and a plate of bread and butter. He places them on the table

Bess (*smiling and indicating the table*) I suppose I *will* learn in time.
David I'll give you a medal when you can lay it properly.
Bess Some people are far too fussy.
David Now you know what you said the first time you saw it. You said how appetizing it looked.
Bess If I'd known then that I'd be laying it myself one day I'd have kept my mouth shut! (*She moves away a little*)
David I'll be bringing the tea in a minute, so you can sit up to the table.
Bess You've forgotten to do something, haven't you?
David What?
Bess Tie my bib round my neck.

 David grins and goes into the kitchen

Bess sits at the table and serves the salmon on to two plates

 David returns from the kitchen with a teapot. He is humming a hymn. As he sits at the table he closes his eyes and lowers his head in silent grace. Bess waits

What's that merry little ditty you're humming?
David It's a hymn, *Oft in danger, oft in woe*! (*He pours tea for himself*)
Bess Very appropriate, seeing we're just going to eat tinned salmon! Ever *had* fish poisoning?
David (*laughing*) Do you mind? (*He finishes pouring*) Er—what made you go to the pictures this afternoon?

They proceed with their meal through the dialogue

Bess For one thing, it was raining and, for another, I wanted to see the film.
David I want to see it too. I was hoping we might go together tonight.
Bess *Were* you?
David Well, we went last Friday.
Bess H'mm! Nice salmon, this.
David It's a new brand we've just got in at the shop; selling very well, too!
Bess Well, that's nice to know!

There is a slight pause while they eat

David Would you like to go somewhere else tonight—another film?
Bess Why don't you go to the one at the A.B.C.?
David Oh, but you've seen it.
Bess *You* want to see it, don't you? You just said so.

David Are you going out somewhere then?

Bess I had thought of it.

David (*dolefully*) Oh!

There is quite a silence while they eat. Bess is very conscious of David's disappointment

Bess (at last) Oi!

David looks up. Bess pulls a face at him. David smiles half-heartedly

Sulking?

David No.

Bess You're sulking 'cos we're not going to the pictures, aren't you?

David Well—er . . .

Bess Now, look, love, we'd better get this straight. I'm quite happy being here and we get on very well together, but we don't want to start getting tied to each other's apron strings.

David But we're not. I hardly ever see you! You're out at work every night except Fridays.

Bess Yes, I know, but that doesn't mean we've got to go out together every Friday night, does it?

David Not if you don't want to—no.

Bess Look, it's you I'm thinking about—not me. A young lad of your age doesn't want to be wasting his time carting a woman of my age around. It doesn't make sense.

David But I like being with you.

Bess Well, come to that, I like being with you . . .

David Then what's the argument?

Bess There's no argument, love, but—well, haven't you got any friends— friends of your own age, I mean?

David Of course I have.

Bess I've never seen any of 'em here.

David Oo! You don't know what I get up to when you're at work!

Bess Who are you trying to kid—me or yourself? Pour me a cup of tea, please.

David Oh, sorry. (*As he pours*) That reminds me, we'll have to have a new teapot. This one's about had it.

Bess It pours.

David It pours, but it's got a crack down the side.

Bess (*with a laugh*) Oo! You should've seen the teapot Richard Burton used in the film this afternoon. He was supposed to be having his breakfast—you know—one of those real Hollywood breakfasts: orange juice in cut-glass glasses, solid silver teapot and coffee-pot . . .

David How do you know it was a solid silver teapot?

Bess I *don't* know, you soft thing, but it *looked* it and that's all that mattered.

David P'raps one day we'll have one.

Bess (*alarmed*) Hey! Now don't do anything daft, love.

David What d'you mean?

31

Bess Don't go drawing your savings out of the bank—and buying silver teapots.

David (*airily*) Oh, I wasn't thinking about *now*; but perhaps in a year or two—(*with a grin*)—when I've been made a manager, we'll have one then.

Bess (*gaping at him blankly*) In a year or . . .?

David (*laughing*) Can't you wait that long for one?

Bess (*puzzled and perhaps a little troubled*) I dunno. I just can't make you out at all; I can't, honest.

David Why—what . . . ?

Bess The way you talk. 'We'll have a silver teapot in a year or two.'

David Well?

Bess You don't seriously think we shall be here together—like this—in a year or two, do you?

David (*quickly*) Why not?

Bess Look, love. As I said just now—I'm not your mother; I'm only the lodger.

David You mean you might get fed up of—(*he gestures*)—here.

Bess Well, no. I didn't actually *mean* that—but when you start talking about 'in a year or so'—well, it's *possible*, isn't it? Just as you might get fed up of me *being* here.

David I won't—not ever.

Bess (*with a sigh, then a smile*) Listen to nineteen years old talking. Suppose you get a girl, she'd soon have me out on my bottom, believe me. She wouldn't stand for this arrangement.

David (*smiling*) In that case I won't get one.

Bess But what about *me*?

David *What* about you?

Bess Suppose I meet some chap.

David looks at her, unpleasantly startled, for a moment, then he slowly smiles

David Go on! You're joking, aren't you?

Bess (*indignant*) Well, I'm damned! Where's the joke, if I may ask? D'you mean you think I'm too old, for God's sake?

David (*tapping her on the knuckles with his fork*) Mind your language! No, of course, I didn't think that, but—(*hesitantly*)—there—there isn't—anyone—is there?

Bess Not at the moment. But, like every other unmarried female of my age—and younger—I'm on the look-out!

David (*subdued*) I see.

There is a pause. They have now finished their teas

Want anything else?

Bess No, thanks, love. And that salmon was lovely. It tasted more like haddock than any salmon I've ever had.

David (*troubled*) You mean . . . ?

Bess (*with a smile, ruffling his hair*) I was joking, love. (*Annoyed*) Damn!

David Now what?

Bess The next time I do that, just give me a sock in the jaw, will you?

David Do what? You mean ruffle my hair?

Bess (*rising and moving away*) Yes.

David But I like you doing it.

Bess (*after a slight pause; smiling*) When I first left home to go into digs, the last thing my mother said to me was 'Never ruffle your landlord's hair. Your landlady might not understand!'

David (*laughing*) And have you stuck to that?

Bess (*laughing*) There's been no temptation, 'cos, up till now, none of my landlords've had any hair to ruffle. Come on. Let's get washed up.

David I'll get your apron.

David goes off to the kitchen

Bess lights a cigarette

David returns with two aprons, one a frilly one, which he throws to Bess

Catch! (*He ties the other apron, butcher type, round himself*)

Bess puts on her apron. David gets a tray from the side of the dresser and begins loading it from the table, with Bess's help. When the tray is filled, David looks towards Bess, who is near him. He smiles at her happily

Bess What are you grinning at?

David lowers his head and shakes it—obviously meaning 'Ruffle my hair'. Bess smiling, gives him a light smack across the face.

David Bully!

David takes the tray off into the kitchen

Bess clears things from the table to the dresser. While she is doing this there is a knock at the front door

Bess (*going to the kitchen door and calling, not loudly*) Hey! There's someone at the front door.

David appears at the kitchen doorway

I'll disappear.

David Oh, but . . . !

Bess I'll be getting on with the washing up.

David (*protesting*) There's no need for you to . . .

But Bess has gone into the kitchen, closing the door after her

The knock is repeated. David, after quickly removing his apron and throwing it through the kitchen door and closing the door, moves towards the front door

The kitchen door opens and Bess's head comes round it

Bess (*not too loudly*) Psssssst!

David turns

If it's Richard Burton or any man half as interesting—call me in!

33

Bess's head disappears and the door closes.

David, with a half-smile, goes to the front door and opens it. Major Webber, in uniform, is on the doorstep

Major Hullo, David. You alone?

David (*almost grinning—with Richard Burton in mind*) Good evening, Major. Come in.

Major (*entering the room*) Well, if I'm not . . . (*She is aware of David's grin. Not nastily*) And what's amusing *you*? Have I got a smut on my nose, or something?

David (*embarrassed*) No, no. It's—er—nothing really. Just something that . . . (*He pulls up*) Won't you sit down, Major?

Major Thank you. (*She sits*) I thought it about about time I looked in to see how you're getting along. I—I haven't had much opportunity of talking to you lately.

David is about to speak

Oh, I've seen you at the Sunday services, of course, but—you know how tied up I am at those. Not much chance to . . .

The sound of washing up comes from the kitchen. The Major stops speaking when she hears this

(*After a moment*) Oh! You're *not* alone, then? You're sure it isn't inconvenient—my calling?

David (*somewhat embarrassed*) No. That's all right, Major. We—er—we've just finished tea. We were going to wash up, but—that's all right.

Major You're sure, now?

David Quite sure.

Major (*after a slight pause*) Er—how are you getting along with your—your lodger?

David (*ingenuously enthusiastic*) Wonderfully, thank you, Major.

Major (*evenly*) I'm glad. (*After a slight pause*) You're—you're not finding it too—too tying—having someone staying in the house with you? (*Quickly*) I only wondered because you haven't started coming to any of the midweek meetings again. Of course, I realize there must have been quite a lot to do—after your mother—but . . . You're not going to desert us altogether, are you, David?

David No, of course not.

Major We should be very grieved if you did.

David I'm not going to, Major.

Major (*with a smile*) How are you getting on with your music? You oughtn't to go too long before starting lessons again.

David I—I'll try to get along next week.

Major I'm very pleased to hear it.

There is a pause. Washing up sounds are heard again

(*Hesitantly*) David—I hope you won't mind my saying this, but—I was rather hurt you didn't let your room to the young man I spoke to you about.

David (*mumbling*) Oh . . .

34

Major I must say I was dumbfounded when you phoned me the next day and told me you'd taken—someone else.

David (*still mumbling unhappily*) I'm sorry, but . . .

Major I'm sure he would have been so suitable (*After a slight pause*) What made you change your mind about him?

David Well—it just happened that—that someone else came along after you'd gone that night, and . . .

Major (*quietly but pointedly*) After I'd gone?

David looks at her. She returns his look steadily

(*After a slight pause*) Are you being quite honest with me?

The washing up sounds can be heard again. The Major looks towards the kitchen, troubled

Didn't you know at the time I was speaking to you about the room that it was already let?

David No.

Major (*reproachfully*) David!

David Honestly, Major . . .

Major (*After a long look at him*) But you knew there was the—possibility, shall we say?

David (*shaking his head*) No.

Major (*puzzled*) But, at the very time I was speaking to you—wasn't—the lady actually here?

David looks towards her puzzled

(*Quietly*) I couldn't help noticing—there was a lady's handbag—(*gesturing*)—here in this room.

David (*quietly*) Oh, I see. As a matter of fact she was upstairs looking at the room.

Major (*more puzzled*) But you just said . . .

David (*quickly*) She wanted to see it because she thought she *might* be able to recommend it to someone.

Major (*quietly*) But she's here herself.

David Yes.

Major David—I have your interest at heart and your mother was a very dear friend of mine. And I know she would wish me to advise you. I'm worried that you've let the room as you have.

David You needn't be, Major. Bess is a wonderful person.

Major 'Bess'?

David Look, Major, I do assure you there's nothing to worry about. And please don't think she persuaded me to let her have the room. As a matter of fact, it was *me* who persuaded *her*.

Major You . . . ? Why?

David (*quietly and sincerely*) Because I believe she was sent to me.

Major (*puzzled*) Sent—by whom?

David (*after the slightest pause*) Our Blessed Lord and Saviour, Jesus Christ.

Major How can you think that?

David D'you remember, when you came round here the day of Mum's funeral, you said you didn't think it was wise that I should live here on my own, that I'd find it terribly lonely?

Major Yes, I remember saying that, but . . .

David You were right; I got that I used to dread coming home—opening the door to an empty house. I wanted someone here with me—someone friendly—to take away the loneliness—but I knew that it had to be—not just—'anyone', but someone I could get on with and who'd get on with me. After I'd advertised the room—every night I asked God, in my prayers, to send—the right person. And He did. He sent Bess.

Major David, you can't believe that our Blessed Lord . . .

David (*quietly*) If I can't believe He has answered my prayer, Major, then I can't believe in *Him* at all. But I *do* believe.

Major (*distressed*) David—you're so young—young even for your years. Don't you—can't you see it's possible you have been too ready to accept the first person who came along as the answer to your prayers?

David I *knew* before she'd been here five minutes, Major, that she *was* the answer. Don't ask me to tell you just how. I'm not clever at explaining myself, but—just her being here—it made me so happy. The moment she came into the house—it seemed to change somehow—become brighter than I'd ever known it to be. I wish I could make you understand.

Major You're only making me frightened for you, David.

David But there's nothing to be frightened about.

Major (*after a slight pause*) You—you do know where she—the lady— works?

David She's a barmaid at the *Golden Lion*.

Major Yes, I know.

David (*with a little surprise*) You know? You mean you know her?

Major I haven't actually met her. But when I heard she was living here— I made enquiries. (*After a slight pause*) She's older than you, of course.

David Yes.

Major You didn't know her yourself—before she came here?

David No.

Major But—since she's been here you appear to have grown very fond of her. (*Quickly*) That's obvious from the way you speak of her.

David Fond?

Major (*with a quick look at him*) I hope that is all you *do* feel towards her?

David We're wonderful friends, and as long as we can go on being just that . . .

Major David—as your spiritual adviser—and for your own sake—tell her she must leave here.

David (*quickly*) No!

Major David . . . !

David No, Major.

Major Being here together, as you are—you are laying yourself open to temptation.

36

David (*with a little laugh*) Major, believe me, you're getting our relationship all wrong.

Major I'm facing facts, David. You are living here with a woman—older and more experienced than yourself—for whom you have already formed a deep attachment. I don't know how she feels towards you, but I can only see it as a situation full of danger—and I must beg you to end it.

David (*after a long pause*) I'm sorry, Major.

The Major rises

Major (*quietly*) Can I see Miss Jones—speak to her?

David (*after another pause*) No, Major. I'm sorry.

Major David!

David (*desperately*) Major—please—leave us alone, as we are. I swear to you there isn't—and never will be—anything wrong between us.

Major (*after a pause; quietly*) You won't let me see her?

David stands still and silent. There is another pause

(*At last*) Very well. (*Very quietly*) But you can't stop me praying for you—asking our Blessed Lord to convince you that what you are doing is wrong, David, and asking him to watch over you and protect you from your own misguided folly. I shall pray for you constantly.

David stands silent

And—pray for yourself, David. And in your prayers ask God to speak to you and tell you whether what you are doing is right or wrong. (*After a slight pause*) We know, don't we, that He is always at hand, always ready and willing to help us and advise us. We have only to ask, and He will put the answer here, in our hearts. (*After a slight pause*) And when the answer comes to you, David, don't turn away from it if it isn't what you hoped it would be. (*She moves towards the door*)

The kitchen door opens. Bess comes into the doorway

Bess (*at once*) Oh, I'm sorry! I didn't . . . It sounded so quiet in here I didn't know whether David was alone or not. I'm ever so sorry.

Major (*quite normally*) I was just going. I'm sorry if I've kept you out in the kitchen.

Bess (*somewhat awed by the Salvation Army uniform*) That's all right. I was doing the washing up, as a matter of fact. I've—I've just finished.

There is an awkward silence. All are conscious of it

(*At last, with a smile*) David, where are your manners? Aren't you going to introduce us?

David (*apprehensive of what the Major might say*) Oh—er—Major, this is Miss Jones. Er—Major Webber.

Major (*politely*) How do you do, Miss Jones?

Bess Pleased to meet you—er—Major.

Again the silence. David is terrified that the Major might seize the chance to 'speak' to Bess. Bess is very much aware of a 'something'. She looks from one to the other. The Major looks steadily at David. She then turns to Bess and speaks quietly and simply

Major I'm afraid it's a case of 'Hello and good-bye'. I must go now. (*Murmuring*) Good-bye.

Bess (*guardedly*) Good-bye.

The Major moves to the door. David also moves up. Bess moves down to the fireplace and stands facing it

Major (*quietly*) Good-bye for now, David.

David Good-bye, Major (*He holds open the door and continues, almost muttering so that Bess will not hear*) And thank you for not . . . (*His voice tails away*)

The Major lays a hand on his arm for a moment, gives him a little smile, then, as she is going through the door, looks back towards Bess. Her look is not one of disapproval, but she is obviously worried. In the meantime, Bess takes a packet of cigarettes from the mantelpiece, extracts a cigarette from the packet, puts it in her mouth—all done absently—and is about to light the cigarette while turning to face the door. She realizes the Major is looking towards her. She quickly—almost comically—takes the cigarette out of her mouth and hides it behind her back

Major (*murmuring, with a half smile*) 'Bye.

The Major goes

David closes the door and stands by it for a moment in troubled thought. Bess, with her eyes on him, now lights her cigarette

Bess (*having lighted the cigarette*) Oi-oi!

David (*turning*) What?

Bess Exactly. *What*? You tell me.

David I don't know what you . . .

Bess You know damned—I mean blooming—well! It's started, hasn't it? Trouble about me being here, I mean—as if you didn't know!

David Now look, Bess . . .

Bess I sensed it the minute I came through that door. I'm very sensitive to atmospheres; have to be in my job. (*After a slight pause*) What did she say to you—your Major friend?

David hesitates

Go on; tell me, I don't mind. She doesn't approve of me being here, does she?

David (*hedging*) She doesn't understand how things are between us.

Bess You mean she *didn't*, but I hope to God she does *now*. I mean—you *have* told her that we're not popping in and out of each other's beds every night, haven't you?

David (*disturbed*) Bess, don't say things like that.

Bess I see! I shouldn't *say* things like that, but it's all right for (*with a jerk of the thumb towards the door*) 'Sister Anna' to *think* 'em! Is that it?

David She doesn't. I've told her that we're just—friends.

38

Bess And I'll bet *that's* cheered her up no end! (*After a slight pause*) She did come about me, then?

David nods

She knows who I am—*what* I am; barmaid at the *Golden Lion*—apart from anything else she might think?

David Yes, she knows.

Bess You call her *Major* whatever-her-name-is. Does that mean she's a big bug in your 'Army'?

David (*after a slight pause*) Yes, she *is*, here at our Citadel.

Bess How big? I mean—I'm a Catholic—when I remember. Well—is your Major to *you* what a priest ought to be to me? That's what I'm getting at.

David (*murmuring*) Well—yes—I expect so.

Bess (*after a slight pause*) If I was a good Catholic, like you're a good Salvationist, and my priest told me I had to—to do a certain thing, I'd have to do it. (*Again a pause*) Has your Major *told* you to get rid of me? 'Cos if she has, I'm quitting just as soon as I can get my things packed. Has she?

David (*quickly and alarmed*) Bess, you wouldn't?

Bess (*firmly*) *Has* she? I know she doesn't approve of me being here, but—(*more firmly*)—has she told you to get rid of me?

David (*bracing himself, and after shaking his head*) No, she hasn't (*He turns slightly away from Bess, with hands clenched and his eyes closed*)

Bess (*after another slight pause; quietly*) You swear that? Look at me!

David forces himself to do so

'Cut my throat if I tell a lie?'

David (*after a slight pause—the words are torn out of him*) I swear it. (*He turns away*)

Bess (*after a little pause*) Oh, well—in that case—I suppose we just carry on until she does put her foot down, eh? Oi! You! I'm talking to you.

David (*turning*) I know. I heard you.

Bess Well, you might be a bit more cheerful about it.

David smiles at her. Bess smiles back at him, then ruffles his hair

(*Changing the subject*) Well—I've done all the washing up.

David Thanks.

Bess But you'll do it next time, my lad, even if the whole blessed Salvation Army calls.

David (*smiling*) I will. (*He moves away*)

Bess (*after a moment, looking towards him*) D'you really want to go to the pictures tonight?

David (*turning eagerly*) You mean—with you?

Bess Huh-huh!

David (*ecstatically*) Which one?

Bess The Richard Burton?

David But you've just seen it!

39

Bess I could swoon over Richard Burton twenty-four hours out of twenty-four any day.

David We'll have to get a move on if we're going to see the whole programme—and I'd like to see it all.

Bess Oh Gawd! Are you a Walt Disney fan? (*Moving to the stairs*) I won't be a minute. (*Turning*) Eh, if your Major finds out we go to the pictures together you know what she'll say. (*With an affected accent*) 'David—I must beg of you to end this unwholesome relationship.' (*She drops the accent*) Soppy cat!

Bess exits

David, troubled by the lie he has told, stands in thought for a moment, then moves impatiently to the fireplace where he stands slowly beating his clenched fists on the edge of the mantelpiece. He then stands quite still, deliberating, then hesitantly locks his hands and bows his head—to pray, but the prayer will not come. With hands still interlocked, he brings them up to his brow with a violent jerk—then, with something between a little moan and a defiant cry, he dashes across to the door, drags his mackintosh hurriedly from the peg and, as he is putting it on, goes quickly to the staircase door

David (*in a loud, somewhat unnatural voice*) Hey, Bess! Get a move on! We're going to be late!

CURTAIN

SCENE 2

The same. A Sunday afternoon, about three weeks later.

When the CURTAIN *rises the room is empty. There is a knock at the front door which, after a pause, is repeated. Then the door opens slowly, revealing Thomas Armstrong outside. He is wearing a raincoat and carrying a fairly large hold-all type bag. He hesitates in the doorway looking round the room— as far as he can see—before stepping into it. He puts the bag down just inside the room, closes the door, looks round again, then goes to the kitchen door, opens it and looks through it. After closing the kitchen door he is going towards the staircase door, when his eyes light on Bess's coat, bag and very stylish hat which are laid on the back of a chair. He moves over to them, picks up the hat, looking at it curiously. His eyes travel to the staircase door. He is definitely surprised and puzzled. After a moment he gives a half-smile and a low 'wolf whistle'. He replaces the hat, stands hesitant for a moment, then removes his raincoat, hangs it behind the main door, takes out the pipe and tobacco from his jacket pocket, fills the pipe, and with eyes on the staircase door, curiously lights the pipe, then having got it going to his satisfaction—and still looking towards the staircase door— suddenly grins broadly to himself, then crosses to the armchair by the fire.*

Thomas (*singing, just audibly, to himself, as he crosses*)

40

'Following in father's footsteps,
Following the dear old dad'.

He sits in the armchair—still grinning to himself. There is a pause. Then footsteps are heard running down the stairs. Thomas deliberately hides himself in his chair

The staircase door opens quickly and Bess, in bare feet and wearing a somewhat flimsy dressing-gown, comes swiftly into the room. She is moving towards the kitchen when Thomas's head comes round the side of the chair

Thomas (*with a smile*) Hello!

Bess, seeing and hearing him, gives a scream of very genuine fright, and dashes towards the staircase door

(*Not rising*) It's all right! Not to worry!

Bess pulls up by the staircase door

Bess (*not recovered from the shock*) Who the . . . ? Who *are* you? What're you doing in here?

Thomas I won't be so tactless as to ask *you* that.

Bess (*panting*) Cor! You scared the life out of me!

Thomas I did knock—(*indicating the door*)—twice.

Bess (*still not over the shock*) I didn't hear you. I was running the bath. I'd just . . .

Thomas (*grinning*) You're not going into details, are you.

Bess (*puzzled*) What?

Thomas I have a *bit* of imagination, you know. (*He grins at her, then looks meaningfully towards the stairs*)

Bess (*beginning to get his insinuation*) Hey! Now look . . .

Thomas (*with his eye now on Bess's dressing-gown which is rather revealing at the top*) I'm looking—and very nice too!

Bess (*pulling the gown around her*) Who *are* you?

Thomas (*grinning*) I'm David's father.

Bess (*incredulously*) Who?

Thomas David's father. But perhaps he hasn't told you he's got a father. Or p'raps he hasn't even got round to telling you *his* name's David.

Bess (*rushing at him furiously*) Why you . . . !

Thomas rises quickly as Bess approaches him. He grabs her wrists, not roughly, but firmly, and twists her round so that she is standing close to him. One arm goes quickly round her so that she cannot get free

Thomas Rough stuff, eh? Well—suits me!

Bess (*struggling*) Let go of me!

Thomas (*grinning*) Say it as if you mean it.

Bess (*still struggling*) Damn you, I'll . . .

Thomas Your hair smells nice. What you put on it?

Bess (*fuming and struggling*) Just let me get my hands on you . . . !

Thomas Well, if you're all that eager . . . Why not? Let's have a good old ding-dong, shall we?

41

He releases her suddenly. Bess almost falls with the suddenness of the release. She pulls herself together and stands facing him

Bess (*after glaring at him for a moment*) Go to hell! (*she moves quickly to the staircase door*)

Thomas (*easily*) Tell David I'm down here, will you?

Bess (*turning and gaping*) What?

Thomas (*grinning*) And tell him I'm not waiting for him with a strap in my hand.

Bess What are you . . . ?

Thomas (*still grinning*) He *is* only nineteen, y'know—or didn't you?

Bess (*closing the staircase door and moving towards Thomas a little*) Now look, Mr—er . . .

Thomas (*as before*) Armstrong's the name—same as David's.

Bess I don't know what ideas you've got in your head—what you're thinking . . .

Thomas No? Funny that—'cos you *look* intelligent.

Bess P'raps I do my thinking on a bit higher level than you.

Thomas Can you think on a high level about sex? I wouldn't know. Anyway, tell the lad to come down.

Bess (*fuming*) Damn and blast you, he isn't here!

Thomas (*easily*) Now look, I've told you already I'm not going to play hell with him.

Bess (*still fuming*) He isn't here, I tell you; he's out!

Thomas (*beginning to believe her*) Then what—what are you doing here?

Bess (*still angry*) I live here!

Thomas (*big*) You *what*? Hells bells!

Bess (*almost shouting*) I'm just a lodger! I've taken a room here!

Thomas You've . . . ! Are you—married? Is your husband here with you?

Bess Nobody's with me.

Thomas (*gaping*) Well, what do you know? David's let a room—to *you*—on your own?

Bess He has!

Thomas I can't believe it! Look! You and him—don't tell me—you're not living together—*are* you? You needn't mind saying if you are; I'm broadminded.

Bess You're too ruddy broadminded, if you ask me. And in case you've forgotten, Mr Armstrong—that is if you were ever sufficiently interested to notice—your son is a bit on the religious side.

Thomas I knew he *was*, but finding *you* here—well you can hardly blame me for thinking he might've had a change of heart.

Bess Well, I can assure you he hasn't, so you can get that idea right out of your head. He's a good clean-living kid, and as far as I'm concerned, he'll stay that way, so you needn't worry.

Thomas Oh, I'm not worried.

Bess Then you damn well ought to be!

Thomas That's a nice bit of feminine logic, that is! (*With a smile*) Well—it looks to me as if I owe you an apology.

Bess (*calming down somewhat*) It looks that way to me too! Nice thing,

I must say—first time somebody claps eyes on you they take it for granted you're a prostitute!

Thomas (*grinning*) Oh, now—come on—be fair! What about the circumstances? Suppose you'd been me—what would you have thought? I arrive here expecting to find my son all on his own. First of all I see them (*pointing to the coat, hat and bag*), but nobody in here, and then a couple of minutes later down the 'apples and pears' comes an attractive and half-naked woman!

Bess (*drawing her dressing-gown round her again*) I'm not half-naked!

Thomas (*grinning*) Not half you aren't! (*After a slight pause*) Joke over! Anyway, I'll bet you daren't take that off! Go on, I dare you. Shall I count three? No? Ah well! Never mind! Obviously not my lucky day!

Bess (*still trying to be angry, but not succeeding very well*) I'll land you such a clout in a minute!

Thomas And by the way, purely—well p'raps not exactly purely—but as a matter of interest—do you parade about in front of David like that? (*Indicating the dressing-gown*)

Bess No, blast you, I don't!

Thomas (*grinning*) I *thought*! And how long've you been—in residence?

Bess A month.

Thomas Well, well! And—is he still tied up with his Salvation Army crowd?

Bess He's out with 'em now. He always is—practically all day Sundays.

Thomas (*muttering*) Blimey!

Bess And just to tidy things up in that nasty mind of yours; the reason I'm in this—(*indicating her dressing-gown*)—I was just going to have a bath and, not knowing I had company, I came down to get a tablet of soap; so you see . . . !

Thomas (*grinning*) I see you were going to have a bath and that you came down for some soap, but what I *don't* see is—how you ever persuaded that son of mine to take you in as a lodger. That has got me beat, good and proper.

Bess P'raps you'd better ask him that.

Thomas P'raps I had. Anyway—and don't give me that clout for saying it, but—finding you installed here is a—very pleasant—surprise, Miss— er . . . ?

Bess Jones.

Thomas 'Jones'? Sure it isn't 'Smith'—or 'Brown'?

Bess (*with a burst of exasperation*) For the love of . . . ! Do I have to produce my birth certificate now? (*After a slight pause*) There's no mystery about *me*, mister!

Thomas Meaning what? That there is about me?

Bess (*with a shrug of the shoulders*) I've never heard David singing your praises. And the only time I asked about you, he shut up like a clam. So—one can't help wondering, can one? (*Suddenly*) David wasn't expecting you this afternoon, was he?

Thomas No.

Bess Where is it you live? Nottingham, isn't it?

43

Thomas Oh, he's told you that much?

Bess That's your life story as far as I know it. (*Hesitantly*) Have you come over for the day—on an excursion or something?

Thomas (*indicating his bag by the door and grinning*) Doesn't look like it, does it?

Bess's eyes travel to the bag—for the first time. She gives a little start on seeing it. She half moves up to it, then down again

Bess You mean—you've come to stay?

Thomas (*laconically*) Huh-huh!

Bess Stay where? Not *here*?

Thomas I doubt whether that son of mine . . . (*He stops talking as a thought occurs to him*) You know—(*grinning*)—you're putting ideas into my head!

Bess You ought to clear some of the nasty ones out first.

Thomas (*looks meaningly at Bess*) Why not stay here?

Bess (*troubled*) But . . .

Thomas But what?

Bess Well . . .

Thomas Don't get agitated, honey. I don't see it'll make any difference as far as you're concerned, or—(*grinning*)—will it?

Bess You'd better talk to David when he gets back. And not so much of the 'honey'!

Thomas Sorry—honey! You think David might not want me around?

Bess You should know better than me. (*Bess moves around the room a little disturbed*)

Thomas sits watching her and smoking his pipe. Bess senses him watching her. She looks towards him—then quickly away. It is obvious that he interests her

Have you—have you finished working in Nottingham, then?

Thomas Yeah! Packed the job in. But I'll soon get another here, don't worry.

Bess (*dryly*) I'll try not to.

Thomas (*with his eyes on her*) D'you know—I've a feeling I've seen you before somewhere?

Bess Now where could that've been? A Garden Party at Buckingham Palace?

Thomas We are amused! (*Reflectively*) It must've been when I was here last time—when I came over to the funeral. David's told you about his mother dying? In October, it was.

Bess He has.

Thomas It must've been sometime then . . . (*Suddenly*) I've got it! Good God! You're the barmaid in the saloon bar in that pub near the station, the—what's it called?—the *Golden Lion*—or you *were*.

Bess And I still am.

Thomas That's right! I called in there on my way to the train—and you served me, and I remember thinking to myself at the time—well, never mind! (*He grins*) Fancy me remembering you!

Bess And fancy me forgetting you!

Thomas (*grinning*) I asked for that, didn't I? But—does David know where you work?

Bess He does.

Thomas Sure?

Bess I'm very sure.

Thomas And he doesn't mind?

Bess Look! Have I got to tell you again I've only taken a room here? It isn't his place to 'mind' what my job is—so long as I'm a satisfactory lodger.

Thomas (*grinning*) And I'll bet you could be that all right!

Bess (*annoyed, but not really angry*) Oo! I will—I'll land you such a one in a minute.

She moves towards him. Again he grabs her, lightly

Thomas (*amiably*) I shall begin to think you're suffering from a 'clouting complex', the way you keep on threatening. (*Grinning, but looking at her admiringly*) If it'll give you some sort of a kick to clout me, then go ahead and do it. Go on! Let fly! (*He releases one hand*)

Bess (*struggling, but not very hard*) Let me go!

Thomas (*smiling, but speaking softly*) We're almost back to where you came in, aren't we? Except that I know just a little bit more about you, don't I? A little bit—but not much—not enough. (*He takes her other hand again*)

Bess (*still putting up a show of resistance*) Now look, mister . . .

Thomas Tom's the name, short for Thomas. What's yours?

Bess (*still 'struggling'*) Never mind what . . .

Thomas Is it so awful you daren't tell me?

Bess It's Bess, damn you!

Thomas And you're not married—or divorced—or parted? (*He draws her closer*)

Bess No, I'm not. Now look . . . !

Thomas (*holding up her left hand and looking at it*) And not even engaged, eh?

Bess (*again with a feeble struggle*) No! Are you going to let go of me?

Thomas (*smiling and speaking quietly*) You'll be telling me next you're a virgin!

Bess (*again the 'struggle'*) Oo! You . . .

Thomas (*twisting her round to face him, and speaking more softly still*) But I shan't believe you.

Bess (*feebly*) You—you swine!

Thomas (*with passion*) Bess! (*He suddenly kisses her chest*)

Bess No!

Thomas Bess!

His lips travel up to her mouth. Bess struggles for a moment, but she is unable to resist Thomas's ardour. Her arms go round him as she returns the kiss. The kiss is held. Then Thomas's hand begins to slip the dressing-gown off Bess's downstage shoulder

45

Bess (*loudly*) No! For God's sake! (*With a sudden movement she releases herself from Thomas's hold and steps well back*)

Thomas (*surprised*) What . . . ?

Bess You must be out of your senses—me too! What if David was to suddenly come back?

Thomas You said he's out with . . .

Bess He'll be in for his tea soon, and . . . (*With a little wail of desperation*) Oh God! I haven't got it laid yet.

Thomas (*moving towards her*) Bess . . . ! (*He takes her hands*)

Bess No!

Thomas Bess!

Bess Oh, why don't you go and sit down, damn you!

Thomas One kiss—and I will.

Bess (*weakly*) Please—leave me . . .

Thomas (*overlapping*) One kiss—for now.

Bess (*giving it to him*) You—rotten—devil! I ought to be scratching your eyes out!

Thomas (*huskily*) Bess, you're marvellous, bloody marvellous!

They go into a passionate embrace. Then suddenly Bess begins to beat Thomas's shoulders frantically with her fists. She is also trying to speak, but Thomas's lips are pressed up to hers and she is unable to do so. At last, she manages to get her mouth free

Bess (*frantically*) Look out!

Thomas (*still holding her tightly*) What . . . ?

Bess (*struggling to release herself*) It's him! For God's sake let me go!

Thomas (*still holding her; mystified*) Who?

Bess It's David! I can tell his footsteps!

Thomas You're imagining . . .

Bess (*quite frantic as she struggles*) I tell you . . . ! (*More so*) Damn you, you bloody fool, will you . . . ?

In desperation she slaps Thomas hard across the mouth with the back of her hand. The blow causes him to release her immediately. He gives a yelp of pain and the back of his hand goes to his mouth. Bess, released, staggers backwards to the wall, or a piece of furniture

At this moment, the front door opens and Major Webber steps into the room—to just inside the door, which is being held open by David. Both are in their Salvation Army uniforms

As the door opens, Thomas spins round to face it. For a split second he still has his hand to mouth, but drops it quickly as the Major enters. The Major confronted by Thomas, stops dead. She does not at once see Bess, who is out of her line of sight

Major (*surprised*) Mr Armstrong! I didn't . . .

The Major is also out of Bess's line of sight. On hearing her voice, Bess gives a little gasp of dismay and immediately runs a hand over her dishevelled hair, then draws the dressing-gown around her. The Major, hearing Bess's gasp, breaks off in mid-sentence, turns and, of course, sees Bess obviously tidying herself

(*Steadily*) Oh . . . good afternoon, Miss Jones.

Meanwhile, David—who has been holding the door open for the Major—can only gape unbelievingly at Thomas. Bess is—for the moment—hidden from his view. There is a moment when nobody moves, but it is only a moment. The Major is 'at sea' as regards the situation in the room, but it is obvious to her that it is not normal

David, you didn't tell me your father was here. Perhaps I ought to . . . (*She turns as if to go*)

Thomas (*almost overlapping the Major's last few words; quickly and a little too heartily to David*) Hello there, son. (*Quickly, to the Major*) No, no, don't go, Major!

David (*with his eyes fixed on Thomas; completely unbelieving*) You!

Thomas That's right! Me! Surprise, eh?

David (*closing the door; still bewildered*) But what . . . ? (*Hardly realizing what he is saying*) Bess . . . (*He now sees her*) Oh, there you . . . (*He pulls up as he notices her dressing-gown and bare feet. He is bewildered, shocked and embarrassed, but not suspicious*) Bess!

Bess (*with assumed brightness*) I know! Awful, isn't it—catching me like this—*and* your father did too! I'm sorry, David. I do apologize, Major, but you see—I was going to get a bath—and there was no soap in the bathroom, so . . .

Thomas (*taking up the story*) Poor Miss Jones—she came down to get some—just a couple of minutes before *you* arrived—and found me squatting in the armchair. (*To Bess*) Gave you a—a terrible shock, didn't I Miss Jones? (*He laughs a little*) Anyway, never mind. How are you, Dave? (*He moves up and takes David's extended hand and pumps it heartily*) You're looking well. (*Then, to the Major*) And how are you keeping, Major?

Major (*quietly*) Very well, thank you.

Thomas Good!

David (*still acutely embarrassed—also angry, though trying to hide the fact*) Sit down, won't you, Major?

Major Oh, but . . .

David (*almost babbling*) Please sit down while I slip upstairs and get the coat. (*To Thomas*) You'll have to excuse me a moment. (*He moves to the stairs*)

Major No, no. Don't bother about the coat now, David; some other time. I'll leave you to . . .

David (*overlapping the last sentence*) Won't take long. I know just where to lay my hands on it. (*He turns, looks quickly round. To Bess*) Mind if I go into your room for a minute? There's a box in there that . . .

Bess What? No, of course not.

David (*speaking generally*) 'Scuse me.

David goes upstairs quickly, closing but not fastening the door behind him

47

Thomas Sit down, Major.

The Major moves to a chair and sits—looking more or less out front. There is a somewhat embarrassed pause. Thomas and Bess, unseen by the Major, exchange looks—each urging the other to speak to the Major

(*To the Major, after clearing his throat*) Tell me—how do you think he's settling down since his mother . . . ? He's getting over it I hope?

Major (*quietly*) Yes, I think so.

Thomas That's fine. Doesn't do to brood, eh?

Major No.

Thomas (*after a despairing look towards Bess*) Er—how's he getting on with his cornet playing? Got him in the band yet?

Major That takes time—and lots of practice.

Thomas Yes. Yes, I suppose so.

There is another awkward pause. Thomas runs his finger round the inside of his collar

Er—quite a surprise to me when I found Miss Jones here. David never said anything—not after the funeral—about taking anyone in—at least I don't remember . . .

Major I think he found it terribly lonely, living here on his own.

Thomas H'm! We were afraid of that, weren't we? (*With a grin at Bess behind the Major's back*) Well, I'm sure Miss Jones'll keep him out of the doldrums. What do you say, Miss Jones?

Bess (*after a glare at him; coming forward*) What I say is it's time I made myself respectable, and I will as soon as David comes down. I don't know what you must think, Major, coming in and finding me like—like Lady Godiva—but I do assure you . . .

Thomas (*grinning*) But Lady Godiva didn't wear anything at all, did she—except a horse?

Bess Mr Armstrong, please!

Thomas Sorry. Have I put my foot in it? Sooner Dave comes down the better.

Bess Yes. And when he does I think I'll have a word or two to say to him. (*To the Major*) I mean—he might've let me know you'd be coming back with him.

Major Oh, but he didn't know . . .

David appears in the staircase doorway carrying an overcoat. He pulls up short. He is by now very much on edge. He stands by the door for a moment—aware of awkwardness in the room

The Major, on David's entrance, rises thankfully. She sees his looks at the others and is, of course, very aware of a 'something'

David (*moving to her*) Here we are, Major. (*He tries to smile as he speaks*) I think it should be all right. It's a bit shabby, but there's a lot of wear in it yet.

Major (*hardly conscious of what she is saying*) Oh, thank you, David, but you shouldn't have troubled about it now.

David (*cutting in*) I'll wrap it up for you. I've got some brown paper here. (*He goes to a drawer in the dresser*)

Major Don't bother. I can take it as it is.

David (*putting the coat over the back of a chair*) It's started to rain. It'll get wet. (*He searches in the drawer, then turns and speaks somewhat abruptly to Bess*) Bess, have you used the big sheet of brown paper I put in here on Friday?

Bess (*aware of and surprised at the abruptness*) What? Brown paper? Oh, yes. I remember . . .

Major (*taking the coat from the chair back*) David, it doesn't matter . . .

David (*suddenly snapping*) It does matter! You don't want to get the thing soaked, do you? (*Snatching the coat*) Give it to me. I'll find something.

Major (*stunned by his manner*) David!

David goes quickly and angrily into the kitchen, taking the coat with him

The Major stands looking after him, hurt

Bess (*after a slight pause*) The young—monkey! Snapping at you like that, Major. He wants his ears boxing!

Thomas That's right. A good clout works wonders sometimes. (*Grinning*) Eh, Miss Jones?

Bess (*after a glare at Thomas*) It isn't like him to . . . All the time I've been here I've never known him snap like that. I'm sure he didn't mean it, Major.

Major Of course he didn't.

Bess But I should box his ears all the same!

David comes in from the kitchen carrying a small shopping bag. He is still distrait but not angry. Towards the Major he is very contrite

David (*after silently handing the bag to the Major, and a quick look towards Bess and Thomas; speaking in a subdued voice*) It's beginning to rain hard now. Hadn't you better wait a bit?

Major (*quite normally*) No, thank you. I'll be all right.

Bess Look! Let me lend you an umbrella.

The Major moves to the door, followed by David

Major (*as she goes*) No—please, I shall be home in three or four minutes. (*To Bess and Thomas*) Good-bye.

David (*muttering*) Major, I'm sorry I spoke to you as I . . .

Bess (*to the Major*) Aren't you going to—(*she gestures 'box his ears'*) . . . ?

Major (*after smiling quite genuinely at Bess*) Doesn't the Bible tell us we should turn the other cheek? (*Turning to David*) 'Bye David, and thank you for the coat. I know it will be appreciated.

After a 'good-bye' smile at the others, the Major exits

David, after closing the door behind the Major, notices Thomas's bag. He looks at it for a moment, then at Thomas

Thomas (*with heartiness*) Well, well, well! After all that caffuffle!

Bess David, I'm ashamed of you. The way you spoke to that nice woman!

David is silent—his anger is returning

What upset you? Was it finding me like this? (*After a slight pause*) I'm sorry, if it was. But surely she'd understand? I know she's Salvation Army—and I suppose a bit strait-laced, but after all—I was only going to have a bath.

Thomas And even *they* bath sometimes, don't they?

Bess (*turning to David*) I'll only be five minutes. (*She goes towards the stairs*) And don't bother about laying tea. I'll do it when I come down. You just sit down and talk to your father.

Bess exits upstairs, closing the door

Thomas stands looking appreciatively after her for a moment, then pulls himself up with a little start. David watches him

Thomas (*moving to the armchair by the fire*) Well, I must say—it was a bit of a shock finding—(*gesturing with his pipe towards the stairs*)—her here. Mind you, I think it was a good idea—taking a lodger, but—(*he grins at David knowingly*)—by Jove . . . !

David (*quietly*) What are you . . . ? Why have you come here?

Thomas (*after a look at him*) I've packed in my job at Nottingham. (*After a slight pause*) P'raps it's old age creeping up on me, but I got sick of being up there on my own.

David (*puzzled*) On your own? But what about . . . ?

Thomas (*quietly*) I didn't tell you last time I saw you, but—Doris and me have been parted for nearly a year now.

David (*flatly*) Oh!

Thomas Yes. (*With a little ironic laugh*) That's twice I've come a mucker. I'll have to be careful or it'll become a habit. Still—what is it they say? 'Third time lucky', eh? (*His eyes stray to the staircase*)

David notices this

David (*hesitantly*) What are you . . . ? Where will you go now?

Thomas Go? I hadn't thought of *going* anywhere—beyond here; well, not for the time being, anyway.

David You don't mean you're going to find work here?

Thomas Don't I? I thought I *did* (*After a slight pause*) I've nothing in view, mind, but I'll just look round for a day or two, and if I do find something worthwhile—well . . . !

David (*after moving away with his back to Thomas*) Have you—fixed anywhere to stay?

Thomas (*after a long look towards David's back*) No—no, I haven't!

David turns and looks at Thomas. They hold the look for quite a while. Then David, outstared, moves absently up to the dresser, takes a tablecloth from a drawer, lays it on the table neatly, then moves up to the dresser again

David (*with his back to Thomas; quietly*) You'll stay to tea?

Thomas (*with sarcasm*) Oh, I *can* stay to tea, can I? Thanks—son!

David (*turning quickly; with a little burst*) It wouldn't work—you living here; you know it wouldn't!

50

Thomas Why not? (*Glancing towards the stairs*) Oh, you mean—'Three, three, never agree'. Is that it?

David I wasn't thinking of—Miss Jones.

Thomas (*with an irritable burst*) You were calling her 'Bess' a few minutes ago. What the hell are you calling her 'Miss Jones' for now? And if it isn't because of her—why wouldn't it work?

David Because . . .

Thomas Well, go on—say it. Because what?

David You and me—we wouldn't get on together—you know that. We've nothing—not a thing in common.

Thomas For God's sake! I'm your father, aren't I?

David (*sharply*) No!

Thomas What?

There is a slight pause

David I stopped thinking of you as my father years ago.

Thomas (*derisively*) Don't talk such . . .

David I did, I tell you.

Thomas How the hell . . . ?

David I'll tell you *how*! When you cleared off—I was scarcely fifteen then, remember—and I saw what your going had done to Mum, I hated you. I hated you so much I used to shout it at the top of my voice sometimes. But when she could think straight again, Mum took me in hand. She told me—kept drumming it into me—that I wasn't to hate you—that it was wrong to hate you—to hate anybody, but that I was to pray for you . . .

Thomas (*with almost a roar of exasperation*) Don't give me that balls! Pray for . . . ! (*Glaring at David*) God! You make me want to vomit! (*Shouting*) I don't want you or anybody else praying for me!

David You needn't worry—not as far as I'm concerned; I *don't*; I never *did*. I couldn't bring myself to do it—not ever. What I did do was make up my mind to forget you—and—over the years—I've managed to do that. You don't mean anything to me now.

Thomas (*blustering*) What?

David You're not my father; you're just *somebody*—and—I'm sorry, but you're somebody I don't want staying here.

Thomas (*spluttering*) You—you—you lousy—sanctimonious—hypocritical—'Jesus-loves-me' bastard!

David (*suddenly shouting*) Shut up!

Thomas (*raging*) Don't you tell me to . . .

David Please—get out of here!

Thomas Not before I've told you a thing or two, you mealy-mouthed little sod!

David (*clapping his hands over his ears*) I don't want to listen . . .

Thomas (*rushing to David, dragging his hands from his ears and holding them down at his side*) You're going to listen, whether you want to or not. When I went off I didn't bloody well leave you and your mother to starve, did I? Not like plenty of chaps in my place would've done?

I sent money every week to keep her and you—*and you*! And, what's
more, your mother didn't have to go to court to get it out of me. I
sent it of my own free will. *And* I left you a home to live in, didn't I?

David But you cleared off; you left Mum.

Thomas Yes, I left her. And if you want to know why—'cos I'm damn
sure she never told you—she drove me to it.

David You went off with a woman!

Thomas Your mother had got me into such a state I'd've gone off with a
bloody tom-cat just to get away! By the time I left her, your mother
wasn't a wife to me any more—a wife!—she was hardly a human being!
Just a prayer-spouting, hymn-singing, tambourine-banging maniac—
that's what she was!

David (*wildly*) Shut-up! (*He shakes his head violently—his hands still pinned
at his side by Thomas*) You're evil . . .

Thomas (*almost overlapping; freeing David's hands*) *That's* what she was,
I tell you. And from what I can see, you're going the same bloody
way! (*He moves a little away*)

David What I am—what I do is no concern of yours! You're nothing to
me! Nothing!

Thomas (*turning violently and rushing at him again*) Don't keep saying
that! I'm your father!

David *No!*

Thomas (*grabbing one of David's arms and twisting it behind his back*)
Damn and blast you to hell—*I'm your father!*

David (*writhing in agony*) No!!

Thomas You . . . (*He twists David's arm more*)

David cries out in agony

(*Shouting*) I'm your father. And you're going to say so!

David *No!!!*

Again a twist from Thomas and a cry from David

Thomas *Say it!!!*

David shakes his head violently

You'll call me father or I'll break your arm for you!

Thomas gives another twist. David cries out in pain

*The staircase door opens and Bess, again in dressing-gown but obviously
wet from the bath, rushes in*

Bess (*topping David's cries of agony*) What the hell's going on in . . . ?
(*Taking in the situation; with a shout, crossing to Thomas*) Leave him
alone! For God's sake, what are you trying to do—break his arm?
(*She tugs at Thomas*)

Thomas (*not looking at her, but concentrating on David*) I'll break his
bloody neck if he doesn't. Go on! Say it!

David I won't! I won't! ⎫
Bess Say what . . . ?   ⎬(*Speaking together*)
                            ⎭

David gives another scream as Thomas twists

52

(*Shouting*) If you don't let him go, I'll . . . ! (*She struggles with Thomas*)

Thomas (*almost overlapping*) You keep out of this! (*He pushes Bess sharply away with his body*) I'm going to teach this young bastard . . .

Bess falls back against the dresser. Fully aware of what she is doing, she picks up a solid-looking vase. Meanwhile, Thomas is again twisting David's arm. David is shouting with pain

(*Shouting*) Say it! Go on, blast you, *say it*!

Bess rushes towards Thomas and brings the vase down on his head. Thomas's grip on David gives as he crumples to the floor. Released, David, almost fainting, staggers to the table and collapses over it, holding his arm. Bess replaces the vase on the dresser. She is panting after her struggle with Thomas

Bess (*panting*) That should quieten him down for a bit!

David is still writhing in agony. Little moans burst from him

(*Coming to him*) David, you're all right, aren't you? I mean, he hasn't broken your arm?

David (*straightening up unsteadily and shaking his head*) I'll be all right in a minute! I . . . (*His eyes fall on Thomas lying on the floor. He stands for a moment, horrified, then crosses unsteadily to Thomas and kneels down beside him*) Bess! Bess! (*In horror*) You haven't—killed him?

Bess (*with a laugh, still panting somewhat*) Killed him? Don't be so daft! He's knocked out, that's all. I'm an expert at that—knocking 'em out! I should be after all the experience I've had! I gave him what we call the 'Golden Lion Special'! (*Derisively*) Killed him? Ha! (*Then with a sudden yelp of panic*) My God! I haven't—*have* I?

As Bess rushes across to find out—

the CURTAIN *falls*

ACT III

The same. Early evening, two days later.

Before the CURTAIN *rises, blasts from David's cornet can be heard. It is obviously being played by someone who has no knowledge of the instrument at all.*

After a moment or two, the CURTAIN *rises. The room is looking definitely untidy. An opened newspaper is on the floor, cushions, unplumped, are 'any old how' on the chairs. The table is laid for tea, but the tablecloth is very much askew. The flowers are not on the table, and it looks a mess, particularly so as two of the three places have been used and the used plates etc. have not been removed. Bess is alone. She is pressing a dress on an antiquated ironing board. As she is in her underwear, we can assume that it is the dress she is about to put on. She grimaces as the trumpet noise continues from upstairs. Suddenly, she slams down the iron and goes to the stairway door.*

Bess (*shouting upstairs*) Look! Do you *have* to?
Thomas (*off*) Don't you like it? (*He blows another single noise*)

Bess slams the door. She returns to her ironing.

> *After a moment, Thomas enters down the stairs. He is in shirt-sleeves with no collar or tie, and wears a 'holy' pair of carpet slippers. He goes over to the sofa and flops into it. Although it cannot be seen at the moment, he has a plaster on the back of his head*

Bess You're a wicked devil, aren't you?
Thomas Am I? (*He blows again*)
Bess You know how David treasures that thing, and how upset he'd be if he saw you mucking about with it. That's why you're doing it, isn't it?
Thomas What a nasty mind you've got! (*He puts the cornet to his lips again*)
Bess (*exasperated*) Oo, you . . . ! (*She suddenly snatches the cornet from him*)

Thomas quickly clasps his hands over his head, pretending he is expecting a blow on it

Thomas (*grinning*) I'm waiting for it!
Bess (*smiling in spite of herself*) Yes, and if I'd any sense I'd give it to you—(*she makes a striking gesture with the cornet*)—only good and proper this time.
Thomas (*rubbing the back of his head gingerly*) You didn't do so bad *last* time! (*Giving a little wince*) Ooh!
Bess (*practically*) Look! You don't have to give *me* that m'larkey. There's nothing wrong with your head now—there can't be, or you wouldn't've been kickin' up a din on this. (*She indicates the cornet*)
Thomas (*grinning*) Is that the way to talk to an invalid?

54

Bess Invalid be damned! You could walk out of this house now and you'd be as right as rain.

Thomas I could—but I'm not going to.

Bess (*annoyed*) You don't give the lad credit for much sense, do you?

Thomas (*abruptly*) No. What little he had, the ruddy Salvation Army've knocked out of him.

Bess All right then, what now?

Thomas Oh, I dunno—another couple of days on the sofa, gradually getting my strength back. I think he'd fall for that, don't you?

Bess And after the couple of days—on the sofa—what then?

Thomas (*looking at her*) Well—between us—we might be able to talk him into . . .

Bess 'Between us'?

Thomas (*with a grin*) No, p'raps you're right! The less I say the better. You're the one to do the talking.

Bess But why should *I* . . . ?

Thomas When you want something, it's worth putting yourself out a bit to try and get it—wouldn't you say? (*Quietly*) You want me here, don't you, Bess?

Bess moves to the fireplace, still holding the cornet to her bosom, unconsciously

Bess, come over here.

Bess turns, facing him, trying to resist him

Come on! (*He holds out his arms*)

Bess (*with an attempt at firmness*) Now look—we're not starting that caper again.

Thomas Come on. (*He waggles his hands invitingly*)

Bess (*with a little break in her voice*) Blast you! (*With the cornet still in one hand, she goes into his arms from the back of the sofa*)

They go into a passionate embrace. Thomas makes to put her arm around him, but she is still holding the cornet

Thomas (*growling*) Put that bloody thing down! (*He takes the cornet from her and drops it to the floor*) Bess—you're—Christ! You're marvellous! (*He kisses her fiercely*)

Bess (*just audibly*) Tom . . . (*Resisting firmly*) No! (*Trying to pull away*) No, I tell you! We were nearly caught last time, remember.

Thomas whispers in her ear

No! (*She releases herself from his grip*) If David did catch us . . . (*With a little gasp*) God—it would be awful.

Thomas (*sharply*) Why—why would it?

Bess (*very quietly*) It would.

Thomas Why, provided we weren't—(*he grins slightly*)—on the job?

Bess (*suddenly flaring up*) Shut up, damn you! Saying things like that . . .

Thomas (*blankly*) What the . . . ?

Bess I'll thank you to watch your tongue.

55

Thomas (*with a laugh*) Now come off it, Bess. Dammit, you know what's what. I mean—after *all* . . .

Bess (*still flaring*) I know! *After all* I'm a *barmaid*, that's it, isn't it? I'm different from other women. You don't have to watch your tongue when you're talking to me. You can say what you like—water off a duck's back! I'm used to hearing fellows talking sex in front of me as if I wasn't there, or taking it as a matter of course that I'm as interested in their mucky stories and goings-on as they are themselves. 'No, no! don't mind old Bess! Bess can take it! One of us, aren't you, Bess girl? Always ready to hear a good story, eh?' (*Muttering*) The filthy so-and-so's! (*Her voice breaking*) And you—you're just as bad. You think you can do the same.

Thomas (*not too convincingly*) I'm sorry.

Bess (*sniffing into a hankie*) I don't want your sorrow.

Thomas Well, what do you want?

Bess (*flaring*) I want a bit of respect. (*After a slight pause*) And I want you to get it out of your head that I'm a prostitute, 'cos that's what you thought first time you saw me—that I'm—easy, 'cos I'm not. (*She goes to him, speaking quietly*) I like you, Tom. What little common sense I have, tells me I oughtn't to, but—there it is—I do.

Thomas (*taking her hand*) Bess . . .

Bess (*quietly, almost imploringly*) But—don't take it for granted that I'm here just for the taking.

Thomas (*still smiling, but speaking softly*) You want the tactful approach, eh?

Bess looks at him almost angrily for a moment, but her face softens as she gives a shrug of the shoulders

Bess (*with a wry smile*) I'm sorry I—said my piece just now. (*She moves behind Thomas*)

Thomas (*amiably*) That's all right!

Bess (*still with the smile*) I mean I'm sorry 'cos—obviously I was wasting my breath. (*Her hand goes out, automatically, to ruffle his hair, but she pulls up before her hand has reached his head. After a moment's pause she moves away*)

Thomas, stretched out on the sofa, has not seen this

Thomas D'you ever have to tick the lad off?

Bess (*turning to face him with a little start*) David?

Thomas Yes.

Bess (*moving to her handbag and getting out her nail polish*) I was just thinking about him.

Thomas Were you now?

Bess (*moving to the armchair, sitting, and polishing her nails*) Of both of you, actually. (*With a look towards Thomas*) Chalk and cheese.

Thomas H'm! Well he's the chalk all right, so I suppose I'm the cheese. After all cheese does have *some* life in it.

Bess (*concentrating on her nails*) Yes—maggots!

Thomas (*not nastily*) Bitch!

Bess And what should I have to tick David off for? He doesn't suffer from your complaint, if that's what you mean.

Thomas You're sure he's never tried anything on?

Bess (*wryly*) I think I should've remembered if he had!

Thomas (*reflectively*) No; doesn't give the impression of being a lecher. (*After a slight pause*) You don't think he's a queer, do you?

Bess (*with exasperation*) Has he *got* to be one or the other? Can't you accept him for what he is—a decent, clean-minded lad.

Thomas (*rising impatiently*) No guts! Gutless! (*He gets his pipe and tobacco from his jacket pocket*) How the hell you've stuck it here—living with him, beats me. (*Feeling his tobacco pouch*) Damn! No tobacco!

Bess It hasn't been a question of *sticking* it. Believe it—(*looking across at him*)—or not—(*looking back to her nails*)—I've been happier here with that 'gutless queer', and whatever-else-you-think-he-is, than I've been for a heck of a long time. At least he respects me.

Thomas (*almost muttering*) From what little I've seen, I'd say he worships the ruddy ground you walk on.

Bess (*quite serenely*) Yes, he does—and that's nice too; specially when you know he's not just playing his cards . . . But it's the way he treats me—and has done, from that very first night I came here—and you'd've thought, wouldn't you, with him being Salvation Army, that when I told him what I *was*, and where I worked, he'd've had me out of the house like a shot? But he didn't.

Thomas And how long is this platonic honeymoon going to last? For ever and ever, Amen?

Bess (*holding a hand out, inspecting her nails*) Course not. How can it? (*Easily, and smiling*) Once you and me are married . . .

Thomas (*spinning round, almost dropping his pipe*) *What?*

Bess (*with her hand still outstretched, smiling across at him*) Ee, Tom, love! You've gone quite pale.

Thomas Who—who said anything about us gettin' married?

Bess I did; there's nobody else here.

Thomas Racin' ahead a bit, aren't you?

Bess (*with meaning*) I may be racing, but I'm still six lengths behind *you!* (*Smiling*) But don't get scared, Tom. I don't think we will get married after all. Six months of wedded bliss with you and I reckon I'd find myself in the Salvation Army too. (*Suddenly*) Hey! Look at that clock! He'll be back in a minute. (*She blows on her finger-nails to dry them*) What are you going to do?

Thomas What d'you mean, 'What am I going to do'?

Bess Are you going upstairs out of the way, or what?

Thomas (*blustering*) Now listen . . .

Bess (*firmly*) If you stay down here, you'll behave yourself, mind. No picking on the lad the moment he gets in. Understand? (*She puts her nail polish back in her bag*)

Thomas Are you going to talk to him—about me staying on here?

Bess shrugs her shoulders

Are you?

Bess If I could think of one good reason . . .

Thomas Dammit, the fact that I'm mad about you—isn't that sufficient reason?

Bess (*steadily*) You didn't let me finish. What I was going to say was—if I could think of one good reason *to put to David.* And I don't think the fact that you're—mad about me—specially the form your madness takes—'d go down very well with him.

Thomas (*coming close to her*) You want me to stay, don't you?

Bess (*looking at him for quite a while*) Yes—damn you, I do.

Thomas (*his arm going around her*) Well, then . . .

Bess (*starting nervously, and moving away from him*) Though why I—I'll end up a nervous wreck if you do, what with trying to keep you at arm's length—and what hopes have I got of that?—and dreading the door opening and David coming through it every minute.

Thomas (*grinning*) There'll be lots of minutes when there'll be no fear of that.

Bess (*with meaning*) Yes, and of course, they just won't bear thinking about!

Thomas (*softly*) Won't they? (*He flings himself full length on the sofa*)

Bess (*sharply*) Now cut that out! And sit up proper. You don't want to be sprawling out there when David comes.

Thomas (*grinning*) But I thought that was the idea—you know—the invalid, convalescing. You tell him . . .

Bess (*louder*) Take that grin off your face!

Thomas *Now* what's the trouble?

Bess You are! (*Quieter*) It's all right for you, making up lies. But it's me that's got to tell 'em, so you can afford to grin, can't you. (*She moves below the sofa*)

As she passes Thomas slaps her bottom

(*Grimacing*) Oh, belt up! (*She snatches the dress from the ironing board and starts to put it on*)

Thomas (*after watching her for a moment*) Bess . . .

Bess Now what?

Thomas Suppose the lad won't let me stay on . . .

Bess Well?

Thomas Would you leave here?

Bess (*not understanding*) Would I . . . ? (*Realizing*) You mean—with you, of course?

Thomas Of course with me.

Bess Living together. After we've known each other—how long—three days?

Thomas Three days—three months—what the hell!

Bess If you'd had your way you'd've had me there and then, the very first day, just like that—(*she snaps her fingers*)—wouldn't you?

Thomas (*gruffly*) All right. I would've.

Bess (*quietly*) Yes—that first afternoon—and—afterwards you'd've been perfectly happy to've had your tea and gone off and found digs somewhere and—and *then* just come along and pick me up at the *Lion* whenever you felt that way. Yes?

Thomas (*growling*) What's the use of talking about what might've . . .

Bess Would you be satisfied if it were that way—if we made it that way now?

Thomas (*after a slight pause*) You mean—you stay on here, and me live somewhere else?

Bess And I did mention you coming along to the *Lion* remember?

Thomas No. I wouldn't want it that way.

Bess Why not?

Thomas I'd want you to come away with me.

Bess (*reflectively*) Leave David . . .

Thomas There's no reason why you shouldn't, is there?

Bess (*still reflectively*) Leave David, and live with you somewhere in the town—yes?

Thomas Yes.

Bess Why, Tom?

Thomas *Why?* Dammit, isn't it obvious?

Bess Tom, I'm not kidding myself that you're—in love with me.

Thomas Look! We're not a couple of kids.

Bess (*as if he hadn't spoken*) And I know damn well you'd be satisfied with the occasional ding-dong rather than us living together—if it wasn't for *one* thing.

Thomas Go on—I'll buy it. What?

Bess (*quite straightly*) David.

Thomas (*irritably*) Where does he come into it?

Bess Isn't he the reason why you're talking about me going off with you?

Thomas (*after a pause*) I suppose *you* know what *you're* talking about.

Bess And so do you! Don't come it with me, Tom. (*After a slight pause*) You said a minute ago that we're not kids. We aren't, not in years, but there's a hell of a lot of the school-kid left in you. You couldn't admit it if you were beaten. You couldn't bear to be beaten and above all by your own son. David's shown you pretty plainly that he doesn't want you here, and—not being wanted—that's a heck of a blow to your pride, isn't it?

Thomas Wasting your time behind a bar, aren't you? You ought to go in for being a psychiatrist.

Bess I can see through you anyway, my lad. You can't bear seeing David happy, can you?

Thomas Don't talk . . . !

Bess You think he's gutless—you said so—and next door to being a religious maniac, and you despise him for it: *and* I think you even despise him 'cos he hasn't tried anything on with me. You can't understand him being fond of me, the way he is, without wanting to get into bed with me. In your eyes that doesn't make him 'good'; just weak and soppy. But what really gets your goat is the fact that, weak and soppy though he may be, he's *happy*; a damn sight happier, I'll bet, than you've ever been in your life, Tom. And that riles you, doesn't it? And there's a devil inside you egging you on to put a stop to his happiness—and *that's* why you'd want me to come away with you, isn't it?

Thomas Finished?

Bess Not quite—d'you mind? You've seen for yourself how well him and me get on together. There's real friendship between us. And if you can't get your own way—if you can't stay on here, you'd like to smash that friendship to bits, 'cos you know that if you managed to do that, you'd succeed in doing what—really—you want like hell to do—hurt the kid, *really* hurt him, and knock all the happiness out of him.

There is a pause

Thomas So what all this rigmarole boils down to, I suppose, is that—if I *have* to go, you're not coming with me.

Bess (*quietly*) No, Tom, I'm not.

Thomas I see. (*Quickly*) And that's a bloody lie. I don't see at all. I don't see what your game's been this last three days—pretending you were—what was it you said—*fond* of me.

Bess You big stupid ape! There was no pretence about it. I am fond of you!

Thomas (*with exasperation*) For God's sake . . . !

Bess I know! That's what I keep asking myself—'For God's sake, Bess, why? What do you see in him?'

Thomas (*with a little sneer*) And what do you answer yourself?

Bess (*quietly*) I've never dared, so far, but I suppose I've got to, sooner or later, so here goes. (*Quieter still*) I've never wanted anyone—so much as I want you—not in all my life. From that first time I saw you . . .

Thomas Bess . . . (*He takes her in his arms*)

Bess (*with a little sob*) I—I couldn't help myself.

Thomas Then what the hell! If I have to go—promise you'll come too.

Bess No.

Thomas Bess . . .

Bess No! Much as I want you, I wouldn't do that.

Thomas (*breaking away*) God dammit . . . !

Bess If there was just myself to think about I would, Tom, honest. I'd come away with you this minute, even though I know there wouldn't be a cat in hell's chance of it lasting—our being together—not for more than a few weeks. But David—I wouldn't hurt him. I wouldn't leave him here on his own, knowing that . . . For God's sake, Tom, can't you see? I couldn't do a thing like that!

Thomas So if he chucks me out—it's the finish between us. Is that it?

Bess But why should it be the finish? Tom, so long as you'd give me your solemn word that David'd never know—and you'd have to do that—I'm prepared for us to meet whenever you like. You could always pick me up at the *Lion* . . .

Thomas Not from Liverpool, I couldn't.

Bess (*gaping at him*) Liverpool?

Thomas (*with simulated surprise*) Oh, of course, I've never mentioned this, have I? I've been offered a good job at Liverpool.

Bess (*still gaping*) But—Tom . . .

Thomas I knew about it, of course, before I left Nottingham. I could start tomorrow if I wanted to. If you can't persuade the lad to let me stay on here—I think I *shall* want to.

Bess (*with a little sob*) Oh, Tom . . . !

Thomas Well, there'd be nothing to keep me here, would there?

Bess (*after a pause*) I get it. I see the way your mind's working. David. If he turns you out you know you couldn't hurt him, so—Bob's your uncle. You'd do the next best thing, 'cos you couldn't admit *complete* defeat: you'd have to hurt *somebody* wouldn't you, Tom? So—it'd have to be me.

Thomas You'd only have to say the word, and . . .

Bess I know. I know. But I'd never say it.

Thomas gives a big shrug of the shoulders, and stretches out on the sofa

Thomas Then, if you *do* want me as much as you make out, you'd better get busy on the lad, hadn't you?

The street door opens and David comes in wearing his working clothes and a coat. He has eyes only for Bess. He does not see Thomas

Bess (*moving quickly to the table*) Hello, love!

David (*overlapping*) Hello!

Bess Bit early, aren't you? I was just going to clear the table.

David removes his coat, half turned from the sofa

David (*smiling*) Too late. I've seen it. (*Coming to the table*) Bess! (*With a little laugh*) This is your worst ever! Look at that cloth! And . . . (*He breaks off as he notices the table has been used by two people*) You had someone to tea?

Bess (*a shade uneasily*) Well . . . (*She looks across towards Thomas*)

David's eyes follow hers and, seeing Thomas, he pulls up,

David (*flatly and uncomfortably*) Oh!

Thomas (*also uncomfortably*) Hullo, there.

David (*scarcely audible*) Hullo.

David stands quite still for a moment, as does Bess. Then he moves to the door and hangs his coat behind it. Bess begins collecting plates etc. once more

(*Quietly*) Don't you worry about that, Bess; I'll see to it.

Bess Oh, but . . .

David, ignoring Thomas, gets a newspaper from his coat pocket, and hands it to Bess

David Here's the evening paper; you'll enjoy it. Lots of Births, Marriages and Deaths tonight.

David gets the tray from the side of the dresser and begins to pile used crockery on to it. He does not look towards Thomas. Bess, very uneasy, moves from the table to the fireplace, takes a cigarette packet from it, is about to take one out, thinks better of it, and sits in the armchair. David, while clearing crockery, watches Bess. He smiles to himself, moves to the mantelpiece, takes a cigarette from the packet, then matches from the mantelpiece, and lights the cigarette. He coughs somewhat as he takes it from his lips and holds it out to Bess

(*Smiling*) Here you are!

Bess Oh! I didn't—I wasn't . . .

David You did, and you were. You know you were dying for one!

Bess (*smiling at him*) Thank you, love. I don't deserve it; leaving the table in that mess.

David winks at her, and bends over her inviting her to ruffle his hair—which she does, almost automatically. David returns to the table. Bess gives a quick, embarrassed look towards Thomas, who is lying on the sofa, watching. There is a pause during which David is busy at the table

(*At length*) Had a busy day?

David I'll say! (*He picks up the teapot*) This tea been made long?

Bess (*in dismay*) Oo! You can't drink that. It'll be stewed to old Harry! (*With a wail*) Ooh! And I don't believe the kettle's on. (*She half rises*)

David I'll see to it.

David picks up the tray and goes off with it into the kitchen, closing the door after him

There is a silence. Bess puts the paper down and begins to tidy the room

Thomas (*rising; in a low, but increasingly angry voice*) The young . . . ! Did you see that? I might just bloody well've not been here!

Bess (*with an anxious gesture*) Keep your voice down!

Thomas (*muttering*) Didn't even ask me how I was!

Bess Look! Why don't you go upstairs again?

Thomas You mean now—right away?

Bess Yes. Before he comes back. Off with you!

Thomas But . . .

Bess How can I ask him to think of you as a sorrowing, penitent father, when all he has to do is look across and see from your expression it's all you can do to keep your hands off him?

Thomas Listen! Not so much of the *penitent* father either!

Bess Right. We'll stick to the '*sorrowing*'!

Thomas (*muttering*) The only thing I'm sorry for is that I haven't been able to kick his arse every day for the last four years.

Bess (*amiably*) Yes, I'll tell him that, while you're packing your bag. (*She hands him his jacket and shoes*) Take these out of the road!

Thomas (*growling*) Grrhhh! (*He moves towards the stairs, then turns*) You finished with the paper?

Bess I haven't started on it yet.

Thomas (*taking the paper from the chair*) Thanks very much.

Thomas goes out through the stairs door

*Bess watches him go, with a smile on her face. After he has gone, she gives
a big sigh, moves to the table, straightens the cloth etc., moves to the dresser,
and picks up the bowl of artificial flowers. She is about to put it on the
table when a thought occurs to her. She smiles to herself, puts the bowl down,
and from the back of the cupboard in the dresser, produces a tissue-paper
package. Opening it, she reveals five artificial, long-stalked daffodils. She
quickly whips the old flowers from the bowl, looks round for somewhere to
put them, and ends up by slipping them under the cushion of the armchair.
She then puts the daffodils in the bowl, and the bowl on the table, in the
centre. She then looks towards the kitchen door, hesitates, then crosses and
opens it*

Bess (*calling off*) How are you getting on?
David (*off*) Hullo!

> *David comes into the doorway*

Just waiting for the kettle to boil. (*He looks across at the sofa*) Oh!
You're on your own.

Bess (*hesitantly*) Yes. Er—he's gone back to bed.
David Oh!
Bess Not feeling too good. Shouldn't have got up, really.
David (*brightly*) Oh well! In that case . . .

> *David goes into the kitchen, then returns immediately*

I've turned the kettle off. I'll have tea after you've gone.
Bess moves downstage. David now sees the daffodils
(*Gaping at them*) Good Lord! What are these?
Bess (*cryptically*) Daffodils! Artificial!
David But where did they come from?
Bess Don't you like 'em?
David (*smiling*) They're very—yellow, aren't they?
Bess Daffodils usually are—up North they are, anyway.
David (*grinning*) Did you buy 'em?
Bess They give you one when you buy a packet of *Doxo* washing powder.
David I know they do; we sell it. But I don't like it.
Bess Neither do I; plays hell with your woollens.
David coughs warningly
Well it does. I've five packets stuck away upstairs now.
David Well what did you buy it for?
Bess (*with exasperation*) To get the daffodils of course, stupid! I *wasn't*
going to put 'em out till I'd got six, but seeing I'd made such a mess of
the table tonight . . .
David (*putting an arm round her*) Oh, Bess, you're marvellous.
Bess Thanks very much! (*Removing his arm with great deliberation*) But
you don't have to be so passionate about it! (*She sits in the armchair*)

*David, smiling, moves upstage. Then his expression changes as he looks
towards the staircase door*

David What time did he come down?

Bess (*seeing where he is looking*) Early this afternoon. Why?

David (*after a shrug of the shoulders*) Has he said anything about going?

Bess (*after a slight pause*) D'you think he's fit to go?

David I wish we'd had the doctor to him; he'd've told us.

Bess Yes, and he might've told *me* a thing or two—knocking him out the way I did. Might've had me certified!

David (*coming to her*) Bess. I'm—I'm sorry you had to be dragged into our—family squabble. I . . .

Bess (*with a little laugh*) *Dragged* in? I jumped in! Ee! When I think of it! (*with another laugh*) There I was—lyin' in the bath, and suddenly I heard you yell! I was out of that bath and nearly in this room before I'd got my dressing-gown on! (*With a grin*) Come to think of it, if I hadn't, it mightn't've been necessary to crack him over the head—he might've passed out from shock instead!

David Bess—you are wonderful!

Bess Now don't be daft!

David I—I was terrified that, after that rumpus, you might pack your things and go. You must've been—disgusted (*Looking towards the staircase*) He—he hasn't—bothered you at all, has he?

Bess Bothered me? Who? Your father? How do you mean, bothered me?

David Since he's been down, I mean. He hasn't had you running after him?

Bess Well, I got him his tea, but . . .

David There was no need for you to do that. I could've done it. I gave him a good dinner at dinner time. He could've waited.

Bess I didn't mind.

David Well, I do. There's no reason why you should do it. (*Moving around*) I'm going to tell him he's got to go tomorrow.

There is a slight pause

Bess (*quietly*) David . . .

David Yes? (*He sits on the box fender*)

Bess (*hesitantly*) Now look, love, I don't want you to think I'm interfering in things that don't concern me—and if you think I *am* you can tell me to mind my own business and get out.

David Bess . . . !

Bess Love, don't you think you're being a bit—hard on your father?

David (*firmly*) No! Not after what he's done.

Bess Oh, I know he nearly broke your arm, but he was in a temper . . .

David I don't mean that.

Bess You mean—leaving your mother?

David nods his head

Yes—well—I don't want to say anything to hurt you, love, but, you know, things must've been radically wrong—between your mother and him, and you don't really know whose fault it was that they didn't get on together, do you?

David I was old enough to see for myself. (*Simply*) He isn't a good man, Bess. (*After a slight pause*) He doesn't believe in God.

Bess There are lots of people who don't, but they're often gooder—better —than some who do.

David (*almost to himself*) He doesn't believe in God, and he hated Mum because she did.

Bess I can't think . . .

David (*quietly*) There was nothing—glamorous about Mum, Bess. She was ordinary—plain I suppose you'd say—but she was a good woman— and I don't just mean religious. She took a pride in her home, in bringing me up, and in—(*with a jerk of the head towards the staircase*)—him too, until he hurt her so much—what bit of pride she had left in him, just—died. You've seen him, Bess; you've seen how good-looking he is. He always was, of course, and somehow, as he got older he got more good-looking. (*After a slight pause*) Women don't always seem to do that, do they? Mum didn't. I don't mean she didn't bother about her appearance, she did, but she—aged more than he did.

Bess (*quietly*) I know what you mean.

David (*after a slight pause*) 'Course, with his looks, he always had women fussing round him, and I suppose it turned his head. He stopped taking her out anywhere, and he began poking fun at her—taking the micky out of her whenever he could. P'raps it started harmlessly enough, but it—sort of—grew on him, till it became an obsession, and in the end it wasn't just poking fun. It was vicious—cruel. (*After a slight pause*) I shall never forget when Mum had to start wearing glasses all the time; the things he said to her—mocking her—calling her 'four eyes' and telling her she looked old enough to be his grandmother—and he used to do it in front of me. He seemed to really enjoy hurting her—seeing her suffer. Then Mum began going to the Citadel—the Salvation Army. I think it started as just somewhere to get away from him. But, gradually, she found faith in God. She found that—turning to Him, believing in Him and praying to Him, gave her strength to stand up to whatever (*with a jerk of the head*) he could say or do to her. And that's when he really showed himself up—when he found he couldn't hurt her any more—when she was, sort of, out of his grasp. He tried to stop her going to the Citadel, but he couldn't. He used to shout and swear about the 'Army', and it drove him that mad, that he even used to go along to their open-air meetings and try to cause a disturbance— chi-iking at them, but it didn't get him anywhere. Mum, with her strength through God'd beaten him, and finally, he knew it. That was when he cleared off and left her. That really did hurt Mum, 'cos, goodness only knows why, after the way he'd treated her, but she still loved him, and I think she really believed that he loved her, deep down, but (*with a shrug*) he just cleared off—with another woman.

Bess P'raps, now he's a few years older, he's come to his senses. Some men do; not all, I grant you, but some.

David I don't think he's showing much sense wanting to stay here.

Bess No? Well, I'd say it's the first sensible idea he's had in years.

David Why is it?

Bess Say what you like, you are his son.

David I was his son when he went off and left me—and Mum.

Bess I still say you don't know the ins and outs of that. (*Quickly*) Oh, I know, I know; there was another woman, but . . . (*She shrugs her shoulders*) But he didn't leave *you* on your own did he? You *had* your mother. Now you *are* on your own—and so is he. Can't you believe that, p'raps, you're on his conscience?

David Bess, I'm sure you're . . .

Bess (*cutting in*) Or, p'raps—though he'd never admit it—the time's come when he feels the need to be with someone who really *belongs* to him. And who's he got—'cept you? (*After a slight pause*) He's a lonely man, David. And—and—I know he's behaved badly to you, but what about 'Forgive us our trespasses as we forgive them that . . .'?

David moves away. There is a pause

David But—you wouldn't like him here, in the house, would you?

Bess (*after a slight pause*) It—it wouldn't be any concern of mine, would it?

David Not any . . . ? 'Course it would. This is your home now, just as much as it's mine. You're happy here, aren't you?

Bess Of course I am. But if I thought I was spoiling the chance of you and your father coming together again, you wouldn't see me for dust.

David I'd never let you go, Bess.

Bess There'd be no *need* for me to go, love—or him. If only you'd . . .

David He's asked you to ask me to let him stay, hasn't he?

Bess (*after a slight pause*) And if he has, doesn't that show how much he really wants to? Asking me—a stranger—to plead for him.

David He shouldn't've done that. He shouldn't've worried you.

Bess Think about it, David. Will you?

David is silent

I don't mean right now. Later on.

She goes to him and ruffles his hair. He smiles at her

Hey! Hadn't you better have something to eat? You must be famished.

David I only want a cuppa. I'll have to be going to the Citadel soon, then I'm having supper at the Major's. (*He sees the cornet which Thomas has thrown down and picks it up. Concerned*) What's—what's this doing down there?

Bess (*turning*) What? (*Seeing the cornet*) Oh . . . er . . .

David Has—he (*with a jerk of his head*) been mucking about with it?

Bess He was trying to play it while I was upstairs getting washed.

David stands, holding the cornet and looking at it, lost in thought

He hasn't damaged it, has he?

David (*after shaking his head*) Mum gave me this.

There is a silence

Bess (*brightly*) D'you know, I've seen you nursing that; I've seen you polishing it, but I've never yet heard you playing it. *Can* you play it, or is it just to look at?

David (*after a wry smile*) I haven't practised now for weeks. I ought to've done, but . . .

Bess (*with mock severity*) You can't blame *me*. I haven't stopped you!

David If I don't start again soon, I'll forget what I *do* know.

Bess Oh, you can play something? Well, come on, let's hear you.

David (*laughing, embarrassed*) Go on! You don't want to . . .

Bess Now don't start getting all coy. Let's hear if you can play or not.

David All right. But—it'll be a hymn.

Bess I didn't think it'd be the cha-cha somehow. Well, go on. Get cracking!

David quietly and still a little uncertainly, plays the hymn 'There is a Green Hill'. Bess watches him for a moment or two, then turns her head away and lowers it. She sits quite still until the end of the verse

(*A little chokily*) H'm! Not so bad!

David Thanks!

Bess (*with a little sniff*) Ee! I don't know when I heard that last. Not since I was at school, I don't think. I can hardly remember the words. How does it go? (*Singing very quietly to herself*) 'There is a green hill . . .'

David Half a minute!

Bess What?

David (*raising the cornet to his lips*) Start again!

Bess (*protesting*) What? Oh, no, I . . .

David Go on. Have a shot!

He begins to play the hymn again. Bess, falteringly, sings it

Bess (*singing quietly*) 'There is a green hill far away, within . . .'

David (*lowering the cornet a little*) 'Without'.

Bess What?

David 'Without' a city wall; not *within*. (*He plays the line again and on to the end of the verse*)

Bess (*singing*) 'Without—'

She looks towards David, who winks at her

'—a city wall,
Where the dear Lord was crucified,
Who died to save us all.'

There is a moment's pause

David Next verse?

Bess (*almost with a yelp*) No! Apart from the fact I don't know it, you'll have me roaring my eyes out! (*She produces a handkerchief and blows her nose noisily*) Go on! (*Indicating the cornet*) Put it away and get your tea.

David (*as he puts the cornet in its box. Quietly*) Bess, *you* believe in God, don't you?

Bess (*embarrassed*) Why yes—of course.

67

David Do you say your prayers?

Bess (*protesting*) Now look . . . !

David (*coming to her and speaking quite simply*) If I didn't say mine, *you* wouldn't be here.

Bess What?

David You wouldn't. When I decided to let your room, I was scared as to who I'd get. I used to ask God, in my prayers, to send someone—y'know—nice. (*Squatting on his haunches beside her*) And he did; he sent you.

Bess knows she is near to tears. She deliberately becomes mock angry

Bess (*giving David a push which sends him sprawling on the floor*) Look! If you don't go and get yourself that cup of tea I'll give you such a clout!

David (*moving to the kitchen door*) O.K.!

Bess And what time will you be back tonight—after your high jinks at the Major's I mean?

David I'll be home before you. Shall I come and meet you?

Bess Think you'll be sober enough? In any case, I'm off duty tonight.

David (*turning*) What?

Bess Yes. One of the other barmaids asked me if I'd swap duties with her. She wants to go somewhere Friday night.

David (*boyishly hurt*) But you never told me at breakfast.

Bess (*with good-natured exasperation*) She didn't ask me till lunchtime today.

David If I'd known I wouldn't've . . . I *could* get out of going. I . . .

Bess (*putting one hand on his shoulder and wagging the other at him authoritatively*) You're going to that meeting my lad, and you're going to the Major's afterwards.

David But what about you? What will you do?

Bess Sit on the doorstep sobbing my heart out till you come back.

David No, but seriously, Bess. What *will* you do? You won't stay in with (*jerking his head towards the staircase*) him?

Bess I shall go to the pictures. Frank Sinatra's at the Odeon. Oo! What that man does to me!

David (*laughing in spite of himself*) Richard Burton—Frank Sinatra . . .

The staircase door opens and Thomas appears

Bess (*seeing him; uncomfortably*) Oh!

David looks at Thomas but does not speak

I—I thought you'd gone back to bed.

Thomas (*easily*) No, no; just lying on it, that's all. I heard the—the music. (*To David; affably*) First time I've heard you. Sounded good. You've got a nice touch or—or blow—or whatever you er . . .

David (*quietly*) Thanks.

Thomas (*affably*) 'Course, they do say 'Distance lends enchantment . . .', don't they? (*He grins affably*) No, actually I came down for my tobacco. (*Moving to the table*) Now, where did I . . . ? Ah, yes! Here it is. (*He*

68

feels his pouch) Damn! I meant to ask one of you to get me some more. Only a couple of pipefuls left.

Bess All the shops round here'll be shut by now.

Thomas Dammit.

There is a slight pause

David (*hesitantly*) There's a shop in the High Street'll be open—doesn't shut till eight. I can bring some back with me if you like.

Thomas is very much aware of David's somewhat more friendly tone

Thomas (*after a slight pause*) You goin' out tonight, then? Oh well—thanks. Thanks very much.

David (*quietly*) That's all right.

Thomas (*handing some money to David*) Get me an ounce, will you? Three Nuns.

Bess (*unable to resist it*) Three *what*?

Thomas (*turning with a half grin at Bess*) Nuns.

Bess is about to make a caustic remark, but checks, swallows hard, and moves to the kitchen door

Bess (*to David*) I'll go and make you that cup of tea. (*With a half glance towards Thomas*) I think I could do with one too! (*As she goes through the kitchen door; muttering*) Three Nuns!

Bess exits to the kitchen

David (*going to the kitchen door*) Bess, there's no need for you to—I can do it.

Thomas (*easily*) Leave her alone, lad, leave her alone. Women are never so happy as when they're runnin' after their menfolk. Haven't you found *that* out yet? (*He smiles at David*)

David gives him a half smile back

But of course, if you want an excuse to get away from me . . . ?

David (*shaking his head*) No.

There is a pause

Thomas (*at length; quietly*) Can I speak?

David (*not quite grasping*) What?

Thomas Can I talk to you a minute?

David (*not aggressively*) What about?

Thomas Would it surprise you if I said I wanted to apologize for—for the rough house the other day?

David (*uncomfortably*) Well—yes it would, but—but don't let's say anything more about that.

Thomas (*after a slight pause*) All right, we won't. Forget—and forgive, eh?

David does not speak

(*Aware of this*) Well, forget, anyway. Though—before we do forget it completely—I must say I was surprised the way you stood up to me. I mean, there was none of that 'turn the other cheek' m'larky, was there? If you'd had the chance to land out with your boot or your fist, I reckon you would've done, wouldn't you? (*He smiles at David*) Wouldn't you?

David (*half smiling back*) I might've.

Thomas Good for you. You've more guts than I gave you credit for.

There is a pause

You know, I think havin' Bess here with you has turned out to be a good thing. It seems to've—well—brought you out a bit—a lot, in fact; given you more confidence in yourself. You know, brightened you up. That's her doing I suppose. After all she is a bit more 'cheerio' and has a bit broader outlook on life than your friends down at the 'Army'.

David looks at him sharply

(*Quickly, with a gesture of deprecation*) All right, all right! Don't let's start blowin' our tops about *them*! But—the two of you being here—good friends—well, it must've made a difference, eh? You feel more—more secure now, don't you?

David (*hesitantly*) Well, I don't know about se—...

Thomas (*going on as if David had not spoken*) And d'you know—that's something I've never felt in my life! (*Quickly*) Up till now security's something I've always despised. From the time I left school it was always my ambition to—live dangerously—(*he pauses slightly*)—but all I ever managed to do was live bloody stupidly. Now I suppose I'm getting to the age when a good big dollop of security'd be a very pleasant change; the sort of security you've managed to find, eh? (*Looking round the room; with wave of his arm*) I mean, a reasonably comfortable home—someone to share it with—without complications. I mean there's no question of—sex rearing its ugly head is there? (*Going on very quickly*) *And* you've got your—your 'faith'—your 'belief'. (*Again going on quickly*) And after all, I suppose it's a good thing if you can believe in *something*. One of my troubles's been I've never been able to believe in anything—(*with a short laugh*)—not even myself! (*He pauses, then goes on with a smile*) No, you're sitting pretty—very pretty indeed—or you will be, once I'm off the premises, eh?

David (*uncomfortably*) Bess was saying that you ...

Thomas (*briskly*) I know what you're going to go on about—me staying on here, aren't you?

David Yes.

Thomas (*briskly, but brightly*) Well don't! Don't let's go into that now. Leave it till tomorrow. We'll talk about it then. (*Changing the subject*) Well, now—you're going out tonight, eh?

David Yes.

Thomas (*smiling again*) Er, where are you going? Down to your—er ... ? (*He makes a vague gesture*)

David Yes.

Thomas Yes.

David Then I'm going on to the Major's for supper afterwards.

Thomas (*with a smile*) Good! Give her my regards. She—she lives just round the corner, doesn't she?

David A couple of streets away.

Thomas (*filling his pipe*) Yes. Yes, well have a good time. Er—what time is your meeting over—at the Citadel, I mean?

David Eight, or thereabouts.

Thomas Then you're coming straight back to the Major's place.

David Yes.

Thomas, slowly and deliberately fills his pipe in silence. David stands regarding him for quite a while, as if wanting to—or trying to bring himself to speak to Thomas. He then moves away, Thomas watching him from his eye-corners. David turns and again looks towards Thomas. Thomas gives him a little smile. David, embarrassedly, half smiles back. Thomas again concentrates on filling his pipe

Thomas (*referring to the pipe*) Y'know, I shall regret smoking this now, when I haven't any later on.

David (*after a little pause*) I—er—if you like—I could drop in the ounce I'm getting you on my way to the Major's.

Thomas (*with a smile*) D'you know, I was just wonderin' if I dare ask you to do that. They say great minds think alike, don't they? Thanks, so . . . (*he is about to say 'son' but pulls up*) Thanks. I'll be grateful.

David That's all right.

Thomas lights his pipe in silence

(*After a pause*) Well, it's time I was changing.

Thomas (*amiably*) Changing?

David (*quietly*) Into my uniform.

Thomas Oh, yes. Yes, of course. Special 'do' tonight, is it?

David (*moving to the stairs*) Yes. Tell Bess I'll be down in a minute, will you?

Thomas Sure.

The kitchen door opens and Bess, cup of tea in hand, appears

David (*seeing her*) Oh, there you . . . (*Indicating the tea*) That for me?

Bess That *was* the idea.

David Ta! (*Taking the tea*) I'll take it upstairs and drink it while I'm changing. (*As he goes through the stairs door*) Thanks a lot, Bess. I'll have to get a move on.

Thomas Sorry if I've made you late.

David (*quietly*) That's all right. It won't take me long to change.

David goes upstairs, taking the tea with him

Bess closes the stairs door, then turns and looks at Thomas for a moment. Thomas does not look at her

Bess goes into the kitchen, and returns immediately with a cup of tea, no saucer. She sips the tea for a moment

71

Bess Well?

Thomas Well what?

Bess How did you get on with him?

Thomas (*easily*) Oh, er, so-so.

Bess (*sharply*) You didn't quarrel again, did you? You didn't start picking on him?

Thomas No, no. It was all very amicable.

Bess Thank God for that. (*She sips her tea*) Did he say anything about
your going?

Thomas No.

Bess I don't suppose he said anything about your *staying*?

Thomas I didn't give him the chance.

Bess What?

Thomas He was going to, but I stopped him.

Bess Why?

Thomas (*smiling*) I don't believe in rushin' things.

Bess (*gaping at him*) *You* don't believe in . . . ! My God! That's good,
that is! You hadn't been in this house five minutes before you were
trying to rush me!

Thomas (*approaching her with a grin*) And I didn't do so badly, did I—
not for a start? (*He puts an arm round her*)

Bess (*breaking away; sharply*) Now then! Now then! Cut it out. (*She
moves away, sipping her tea*) Who did all the talking—you or him?

Thomas Me, mostly. (*Easily*) I think I put in a bit of useful work.

Bess (*looking at him sceptically*) I wonder. Anyway, I did *my* best. I said
my piece to him.

Thomas And what did you say?

Bess Don't ask me. My conscience wouldn't let me repeat it.

Thomas Well, between us, I think we've had *some* effect.

Bess (*almost eagerly*) You do?

Thomas Huh-huh! P'raps by tomorrow our—pearls of wisdom—may've
sunk in. (*He grins to himself*) Tomorrow!

Bess (*sharply*) What are you grinning at?

Thomas Was I grinning?

Bess You know damn well you were; like a Cheshire cat.

Thomas I'll bet you wouldn't know a Cheshire cat if you saw one.

Bess P'raps not, but I'm beginning to know you, Tommy lad, and I
don't trust that grin of yours. It generally spells trouble.

Thomas No trouble, Bess, no trouble—not this time. (*He is smiling*)

Bess You mean not for yourself, don't you?

There is a slight pause, during which Bess just stands looking at Thomas

Thomas What you thinking?

Bess You know, Tom, there are times when it's all I can do to stop myself
from rushing straight into your arms . . .

Thomas (*quickly*) Fine! (*He holds out his arms*)

Bess And others when I just look at you and I feel cold shivers running
right down my spine; you frighten me that much.

72

Thomas (*suddenly irritable*) Don't talk so bloody daft!

Bess still looks at him, then, after shrugging her shoulders, is about to sip more tea

Bess Would *you* like a cup of tea?

Thomas No.

Bess There's plenty in the pot.

Thomas It can damn well stay there.

Bess Oo! The charm of the man!

Bess finishes the tea, takes her cup off into the kitchen, and returns immediately

Thomas You're—you're not going to the *Lion* tonight, I think you said?

Bess I did say.

Thomas What are you going to do then?

Bess (*after a look towards him*) I'm going to the pictures.

Thomas (*with scorn*) Pictures! (*He moves away and turns*) Like me to come with you?

Bess (*lighting a cigarette*) No.

Thomas Why not?

Bess I want to see the film.

Thomas *Very* funny!

Bess *And* sensible.

Thomas (*after a slight pause*) I meant what I said, y'know, about going to Liverpool tomorrow—if I don't stay on here. (*He indicates the floor with pointed finger. After a slight pause*) So tonight might be our last chance of . . .

Bess Get your facts right—*your first* one.

Thomas (*with a grin*) That hasn't been my fault, has it?

Bess (*after a slight pause*) And you think it'd be a good idea—just in case, like—if we—made a night of it tonight, eh?

Thomas I can't see anything wrong with it. It'd give us both something to remember each other by, wouldn't it, if—as you say—'just in case'?

Quick footsteps are heard on the stairs

Bess (*very sharply*) Look out! (*She jerks her head towards the stairs*)

David, now in uniform, comes through the stairs door

Thomas (*to David; amiably*) That hasn't taken you long!

David half smiles at Thomas, then turns to Bess

David Oh! I've forgotten my cup and saucer.

Bess Not to worry; I'll get 'em.

David takes his mackintosh from a peg and starts to put it on

Half a minute!

David What?

Thomas sits and watches the two of them

Bess You want a brush down. There's dust an inch thick on your

73

shoulders. (*She gets a clothes brush from the dresser drawer*) Stand still
and I'll . . . (*She begins to brush his uniform. As she is brushing his shoulders, she stops*) Oi! Oi! (*She smiles*)

David What?

Bess (*removing a long hair from one shoulder and holding it out for inspec-
tion*) So she's a redhead, is she?

David Eh?

Bess (*holding out the hair*) Look! On your shoulder, my lad!

David (*grinning*) I wonder how that got there.

Bess I can think of a way. (*She continues brushing*)

It is obvious to Thomas that he is completely forgotten

David The only redhead *I* know is Mrs Matthews.

Bess Mrs . . . ?

David Yeh—down at the Citadel. She plays the harmonium.

Bess And I'll bet she plays some ruddy funny notes when you're around!
(*Straightening up*) Right! Off you go! (*She whacks his behind with the
brush, then puts it back in the drawer*) Off to your meeting.

David Thanks, Bess.

Bess (*smiling*) And say a prayer for me.

David (*grinning*) I will.

Bess *And* for Mrs Matthews—if I get my hands on her!

David (*coming to her and putting on his mac*) Jealous?

Bess (*ruffling his hair*) What's the point? You can't compete with a redhead—not when you're a bottle-blonde.

David (*moving to the door*) See you later, then.

Bess 'Bye!

David is going through the door, oblivious of Thomas

Thomas (*aware of this, but trying not to show annoyance*) Aren't you wanting this with you? (*He indicates the cornet case with his foot*)

David (*vaguely*) What? Oh no, not tonight. (*He hesitates in the doorway,
then speaks, taking in Thomas*) See you later, then.

Thomas gives a brief wave of his hand

(*To Bess*) Remember me to Frank Sinatra!

David goes

*Thomas, an angry expression on his face, rises and moves impatiently. Bess
sees this. She smiles to herself. Thomas, seeing Bess smile, flings himself
on to the couch*

Thomas (*muttering*) Bloody Hell!

Bess moves down and puts her hands on his shoulders from behind the couch

Bess (*half sympathetically, half laughing*) Poor Tom!

Thomas (*rudely*) Oh, shut up! (*After a grunt*) God! It makes me sick!

Bess You mean, the way the lad and me—carry on?

Thomas And it's all bloody pretence—I don't care what you say.

Bess It isn't, y'know.

Thomas (*fuming*) You're both pretending—*both* of you! *And* you both know it; putting on a—a sort of 'cross-talk act' and trying to kid yourselves that all there is between you is a beautiful, buttercups and daisies friendship!

Bess That's all there is—friendship.

Thomas (*shouting*) Don't give me that! (*Grabbing her wrist*) If he asked you, you'd go to bed with him, wouldn't you?

Bess (*trying to release herself*) Tom!!

Thomas (*gripping more firmly*) Wouldn't you?

Bess (*shouting*) No!

Thomas You'd bloody well go to bed with him. And don't try to tell me that isn't what *he* really wants. It's only his—blasted religious mania that's stopping him, and I don't think it'll be so damn long before he manages to say good-bye to that!

Bess (*quietly*) Oh Tom, you're not so rotten as that, are you—that you can't believe there's goodness in anybody? (*Very quietly, not angrily*) Let me go, Tom. (*After a slight pause: again quietly, unemotionally*) Tom—please—let me go.

Thomas releases his grip of her wrist. Bess moves away, almost unconsciously rubbing her wrist a little

(*With a little sardonic laugh*) Lovely sort of life we're going to have together, the three of us, aren't we, if you do stay on—thinking what you do think?

Thomas (*suddenly rising and moving abruptly*) I'm not stopping.

Bess (*shaken*) What?

Thomas I'm clearing out first thing tomorrow morning.

Bess (*brokenly*) Tom. (*She looks at him for a moment then moves away*) Going to Liverpool?

Thomas I am.

Bess (*after a slight pause*) So—he *has* beaten you then?

Thomas stands for a moment, just glaring out front. Then, gradually, a malicious smile creeps over his face. He chuckles quietly to himself

Bess (*apprehensively*) Now—what?

Thomas (*almost amiably*) P'raps you're right, Bess; p'raps you're right. P'raps he has beaten me. (*After a slight pause*) P'raps.

Bess (*still apprehensive*) What . . . ?

Thomas (*with a business-like wave of the hand*) Forget it! Forget it! (*He moves deliberately, as if dismissing the subject*) You're still going to the pictures?

Bess (*after a slight pause*) Yes—I am.

Thomas No use my trying to persuade you? My last night . . . ?

Bess (*turning away; in a choked voice*) No.

Thomas When're you goin'?

Bess In a few minutes.

Thomas (*quietly*) H'm! Well—that's that, isn't it? (*After a move*) And what the hell do I do now?

75

Bess (*hardly aware of what she is saying*) Why don't you go out and have a drink?

Thomas (*looking at her deliberately*) It isn't a drink I want.

Bess turns away

(*After a wry grin; almost muttering*) I'll go and pack my things ready for the morning and then—turn in. No point in sitting down here on my own. I might go stark, bloody bonkers. (*He looks towards Bess, then moves to the staircase door. Turning*) 'Course—if you *should* change your mind . . .

Bess turns and looks at him

(*Opening the door*) I'm only saying 'if'—(*with a big smile*)—don't be afraid to come up (*he jerks his head stairwards*) and wake me, will you? (*After a slight pause*) Will you?

Bess moves a step or two away

Thomas watches her, smiling, then turns and goes slowly upstairs

Bess stands still for quite a long time. She then moves, almost automatically, to the mantelpiece, and takes a cigarette from the packet, lights it, and stands facing the fire as she smokes, lost in thought. Suddenly she gives a 'someone-walking-on-my-grave' shudder. She pulls herself together, moves up and deliberately closes the staircase door. She then gets her coat, puts it on, collects her handbag, moves to the mantelpiece and stubs the cigarette out carefully and leaves it balanced on an ashtray.

Bess then gives a quick look at herself in the mirror over the fireplace, moves to the front door, hesitates, turns, looks towards the staircase door, then, after a moment, turns and goes out of the front door, closing it behind her

The Lights fade to denote the passing of an hour

When the Lights come up again, the room is empty

After a slight pause, David comes through the street door, dressed as when he went out. He looks around—surprised at not seeing Thomas. He comes to behind the table, takes an ounce packet of Three Nuns tobacco from his pocket, puts in on the table, then, on second thoughts, takes a biscuit tin from the dresser, puts it on the table and places the tobacco on top of it, to make it more conspicuous. He then stands rubbing his cold hands for a moment, then notices the gas fire is on. It also dawns on him that the lights were on when he came in. He registers slight surprise, and looks towards the staircase door, hesitates as if to go to it, then moves down to the fire, crouches down beside it, warming his hands, and humming quietly to himself.

The staircase door opens quietly, and Thomas, with his tie hanging loose, his waistcoat undone, his jacket over his arm and his shoe-laces unfastened, appears in the doorway. He looks around, sees David by the fire, comes into the room, after closing the staircase door. He moves silently down to almost behind David

Thomas (*not loudly*) Hullo, there!

David spins round, rather startled

David Oh!

Thomas Startle you?

David I didn't hear you come in. You were upstairs then.

Thomas Yes.

David I didn't know whether p'raps you'd gone out.

Thomas (*fastening his tie*) And where did you think I might've gone?
(*After a slight pause*) To the pictures with Bess?

David (*after a quick look at him; quietly*) I didn't think about *where* you'd
gone.

Thomas, in silence, continues dressing. David is silent also

Thomas (*at length*) I suppose you wouldn't've liked it if I *had* gone with
her.

David (*turning to the fire; after a moment*) I've brought you your tobacco.
It's on the table.

Thomas Thanks. (*He moves to a chair and sits tying his shoe-laces*)

David (*rising*) I'll have to be getting along to the Major's.

Thomas (*eyes on the shoe-lacing*) You haven't answered my question.

David (*hedging*) What question?

Thomas (*quietly*) You know damn well what question. You wouldn't've
liked it if I'd gone to the pictures with Bess, would you?

David I—I don't know why you're asking me. It wouldn't be anything
to do with me. I mean—it isn't as if . . .

Thomas As if what?

David (*with a little exasperation*) Well, she's free to do as she likes, isn't
she? She can go to the pictures—or anywhere—with anyone she chooses.

Thomas (*with a little laugh*) True! True! I'm forgettin'. After all she *is*
only a lodger here. It isn't as if you and her were—married—or anything—remotely like that.

David (*after hesitating*) Look, I'll have to be going. (*He moves towards
the door*)

Thomas (*easily*) How was the meeting tonight, at the Citadel—bang on?

David How d'you mean?

Thomas Lots there? Lots of good hearty hymns you could all get your
teeth into?

David (*moving deliberately*) I'll see you later.

Thomas (*with firmness*) Just a minute.

David I don't want to be late at . . .

Thomas Just a minute! (*After a slight pause*) I have some news for you.

David What?

Thomas Good news. Shut the door.

David (*closing the door and turning*) Well?

Thomas (*quietly*) I'm clearing out tomorrow.

David (*gaping at him*) You're . . . ?

Thomas (*grinning*) Surprised?

David You mean you're—leaving here?

Thomas I'm leaving this town. I'm going to a job at Liverpool.

David (*bewildered*) Liver . . . ? But you've never said anything about . . . When did you hear about it? Is it a good job?

Thomas (*grinning*) Come off it! What do you care what kind of a job it is so long as it takes me away from here?

David is silent

You were quite right, y'know—what you said that first day I came back. It wouldn't work—me living here. I'd just be—an intruder. You're—as I said earlier on tonight—you're—sitting pretty. You've got your home, you've got your hymn singing, and you've got—Bess. Everything you want, really. Couldn't be better for you, could it? There's no room for me, is there, not really, in your—well-ordered life?

David I don't know why you're talking like this. To hear you, anyone'd think you—resented me being happy.

Thomas (*easily*) No, no! I don't resent your happiness. I don't really envy you. And yet—I wonder if it's a good thing being so completely blind to facts—like you are.

David I don't know what you're talking about.

Thomas I know you don't—and it's pathetic that you don't.

David What—what facts do you reckon I'm blind to then?

Thomas (*with a smile*) Sure you want me to tell you?

David Yes.

Thomas Bess!

David What? (*Abruptly*) I don't want to talk about Bess.

Thomas (*quickly*) Why not? Scared, are you?

David There's nothing to be scared about.

Thomas No?

David No. And I don't want to talk about her, I tell you.

Thomas (*quietly, but firmly*) You may not want to talk about her, but it's time you started *thinking* about her—*and* learned the truth about her.

David I don't know what you're . . .

Thomas No! I know you don't! You've been so bloody wrapped up in your hymn singing and prayer spouting you don't know anything about life, folk, or any damn thing else. If you *did*, you'd've known the first minute you clapped eyes on your precious Bess, what any kid in the street, half your age could've told you—she's a whore!

David (*rushing at Thomas*) Don't you . . . !

Thomas (*holding him at arm's length by a grip on his coat*) Oh, you *do* know what a whore is then? Well that's *something*.

David You're lying! You're lying!

Thomas She's a whore, I tell you! She's any man's meat!

David You're lying!

Thomas begins to laugh quietly, still holding David at arm's length, by one hand only. He suddenly releases him, and goes and opens the staircase door

Thomas (*calling amiably, but loudly*) Bess!

David gives a gasp and stands transfixed

78

David (*almost babbling*) She isn't—she's at the . . .
Thomas (*as before*) Bess!
Bess (*off, upstairs*) What is it?

David stands frozen

Thomas (*calling*) Come down here a minute.

David rushes towards the stairs. Thomas grabs him in a firm hold with one hand, and claps the other over David's mouth

Bess (*off; during this*) What for?
Thomas Never mind what for. Come down.

David struggles for a moment unavailingly

Bess (*off*) I'm not properly dressed yet.
Thomas (*calling, with a laugh*) What the hell? You haven't been dressed at *all* for the last three-quarters of an hour!
Bess (*off*) Trust you to . . .
Thomas (*cutting in*) Hurry up!

Still holding David and still with his hand over his mouth, Thomas grins at him. Footsteps are heard coming downstairs. Thomas suddenly throws David off

Bess (*approaching*) Now then, what is it?

Bess, only partly dressed, appears on the stairs

What's all the . . . ? (*She stops dead on seeing David. For a moment she can only gape at him. After a long pause, and almost in a whisper*) Oh—God!

David, after a long look at Bess, covers his face with his hands and stumbles away. Bess, dazedly, looks at Thomas

Thomas (*with a smile*) Thanks, Bess—for helping me to settle an argument.
Bess (*in a quiet voice, full of loathing*) You—bloody—swine!

Thomas's smile expands as he looks at Bess

Thomas (*at length; quietly*) 'Scuse me!

Thomas pushes past Bess and goes upstairs

David sobs quietly into his hands. Bess looks towards him, then moves into the room a little.

Bess David . . . (*After a pause*) David . . .

David shakes his head convulsively. He sags to the floor in a kneeling position, his arms and face resting on a seat. Bess makes a move towards him, but after a step or two, stops

Thomas, with overcoat on and bag in hand, comes down the stairs. He is about to go out through the street door when he turns, and returns to the table and picks up the tobacco

Thomas (*with a smile towards David*) I did pay you for this, didn't I?

(After tossing the tobacco packet into the air he puts it in his pocket and moves to the street door)

Bess *(almost unaware of Thomas, looking at David)* Oh God, help me to say something to him.

Thomas *(with the door open)* Halleluia!

Bess looks at Thomas, who gives her a grin

Thomas exits through the street door, closing it behind him

Bess looks towards the closed door for a while, then back at David

Bess *(at length; almost sharply)* David, look at me! Speak to me! *(Explosively)* Well, for God's sake, do something. Sock me in the jaw—anything, but don't just do nothing. And if you're praying for me, I don't want your prayers, 'cos I haven't done anything wrong. I haven't committed any crime. I haven't taken a father away from anybody, not even from you, 'cos you've always denied he *is* your father.

David rises, moves to the mantelpiece, and picks up the photograph of his mother and himself

(Seeing this) What are you . . . ? *(With firmness)* Put that down.

David ignores her

Put it down! *(She crosses and snatches the photograph from him)*. God! Can't you let her rest in peace? Can't you stand on your own two feet. When are you going to stop leaning on a mother who's dead?

David moves away, covering his ears with his hands

You don't want to hear, do you? You don't want to talk. You don't want to think, but it's time you damn well did. It's time you grew up and realized that life isn't all hymn singing and that sex isn't just a mucky word.

David sits in a chair

What's happened tonight might seem like the end of the world to you right now. But you'll get over it; you'll have to. And by the time you've reached my age, like as not, you'll have a bloody good laugh about it. *(After a slight pause)* You know where you've gone wrong, don't you? You've put me up on a flippin' pedestal where I've no right to be. I'm not one of your Salvation Army women who can get all the satisfaction they want from a couple of prayers to the Almighty. I'm flesh and blood, and I've got all the natural instincts that God put into me, so you tell me where I've gone wrong. Go on—if you're setting yourself up as judge and jury, just tell me where I've gone wrong. I haven't broken any commandments; I haven't committed adultery. For pity's sake grow up, love; get out of your nappies, 'cos if you don't, believe you me, somebody's goin' to boot you out of 'em a damn sight harder than I'm doing now.

David begins to go down on his knees

(Exploding more) And if you go down on your knees again I'll—I'll give

you such a belting you'll never get off 'em again. (*Again exploding*) And for God's sake say something! Don't leave it all to me. (*Moving to the mantelpiece*) I've talked myself hoarse. (*She picks up a cigarette packet and looks into it*)

The CURTAIN *starts to fall slowly*

(*Throwing the packet away*) And now I haven't even got a bloody cigarette. God Almighty!

CURTAIN

FURNITURE AND PROPERTY LIST

ACT I
Scene 1

On stage—Sofa. *On it:* cushions
      Armchair
      Tub chair
      2 small chairs
      Club fender
      Dresser. *On top:* vases, ornaments, biscuit tin. *In cupboards or drawers:* bundle of documents, Post Office Bank Book, spike file, bills, clothes brush
      Occasional table
      Small table
      On back of main door: coat-hooks
      On floor by wall: cornet in case
      On mantelpiece: photograph of David and Mother, clock
      Over mantelpiece: mirror
      Below fireplace: paper rack with copies of *War Cry*
      Carpet
      Stair carpet
      Window blind

Off stage—Tray with 2 cups, 2 saucers, 2 spoons, sugar, milk jug, teapot (DAVID)

Personal—DAVID: Yale key
      THOMAS: pipe, tobacco in pouch, matches, watch
      MAJOR: watch

Scene 2

Strike—Thomas's mac

Set—*On main table:* cloth, bowl of artificial flowers, tea-cup and saucer, spoon, milk, sugar, teapot with cosy, scrambled egg on toast, knife, fork, cake on plate with doyley, cake knife
      On mantelpiece: 2 unopened letters.

Off stage—Cup and saucer (DAVID)

Personal—BESS: handbag with handkerchief and compact, watch

ACT II
Scene 1

Strike—Dishes etc. from main table

Set—General effect of untidiness
      Sofa cushion on floor
      Bowl of artificial flowers on dresser
      Women's magazine, open cigarette packet, lighter on armchair
      Bess's coat on small chair
      Meal for two on main table, less neatly than in previous scene
      Morning paper in paper rack
      Tray beside dresser
      Cigarettes and matches on mantelpiece
      David's mac on door hook

Off stage—Dish of tinned salmon, plate of bread and butter (DAVID)
Teapot (DAVID)
2 aprons (DAVID)

Personal—BESS: make-up
DAVID: packet of 20 cigarettes

SCENE 2

Re-set—Sofa cushion
Untidy oddments into different places

Set—Bess's coat, bag and hat on chair
Tablecloth in dresser drawer

Off stage—Hold-all bag (THOMAS)
Overcoat (DAVID)
Shopping bag (DAVID)

ACT III

Strike—Bess's hat, bag and coat
Hold-all bag

Set—3 meal places on main table, very untidily
Open newspaper on floor
General increase of untidiness
Ironing board, iron and dress by fire
Bess's handbag with nail polish on dresser
Thomas's jacket with pipe and tobacco on chair
Thomas's shoes by fire
Bowl of artificial flowers on dresser
Artificial daffodils, wrapped, in dresser cupboard
David's mac on hook

Off stage—Cornet (THOMAS)
Newspaper (DAVID)
Cup of tea with saucer (BESS)
Cup of tea without saucer (BESS)
Packet of *Three Nuns* tobacco (DAVID)
Hold-all bag (THOMAS)

Personal—BESS: handkerchief

LIGHTING PLOT

Property fittings required—pendant, gas fire
Interior. A Living-room. The same scene throughout

ACT I Scene 1 Afternoon
To open: Window curtains closed, room dim, fire on

Cue 1	David lets up blind	page 1
	Bring up to full daylight	

ACT I Scene 2 Evening
To open: Pendant and fire on
No cues

ACT II Scene 1 Evening
To open: As previous scene
No cues

ACT II Scene 2 Afternoon
To open: Effect of late daylight. Fire on

ACT III Evening
To open: Pendant and fire on

Cue 2	Bess exits	page 76
	Fade to Black-out	
Cue 3	When ready	page 76
	Fade up to previous lighting	

*2284-1
1981
5-07
C.

EFFECTS PLOT

ACT I
SCENE 1

No cues

SCENE 2

ACT II
SCENE 1

SCENE 2

No cues

ACT III

No cues

85

MADE AND PRINTED IN GREAT BRITAIN BY
BUTLER & TANNER LTD, FROME AND LONDON
MADE IN ENGLAND